IN THE ATTIC OF MY MIND

*Random stories from White Plains, Middlebury,
Pentagon, CIA, Dartmouth, Bank of Boston, Lincoln
Canoe and more with family and friends.*

By Christopher D. Van Curan
and Bonzo Serizio

Published by Piscataqua Press
142 Fleet St., Portsmouth, NH 03801
www.ppressbooks.com
info@piscataquapress.com

ISBN: 978-1-944393-77-9

Contents

Dedication

This book is dedicated to Juneta Dinsmore Allen, my mother also known as "Nettie," who before she died in June 1990, thought the title of this book was a good one and my regret is that she never had the opportunity to read it. She was an inspiration to all who knew her, had literary skills and interests I never had and we all loved her dearly. She was a mother that I wish everyone in the world could have.

In June on a clear night we can see "Nettie's" bright star to the southwest all by itself shining down on us.

Recognition

I could not get very far in my writing efforts without recognizing the family talent for writing resided with my grandfather, Regnall Stanford Dinsmore, who wrote many short stories for the pulp magazines of the 1920's, 1930's and early 1940's. Whether any of that family talent transcended to future generations is up to the judgment of the reader – if there are any.

Also, there is Bonzo Serizio. Bonzo is a fictional character who emerged in my life out of occasional necessity. Any father who has stood in a ski lift line with his children has experienced this event. Your child yells out "Daddy" and the 20 fathers in the line all turn their heads towards the yelling child. Nope not theirs was the response of 19 of them. I thought this needed fixing. So I gave me another name, an alias, "Bonzo Serizio ." How many fathers have that name? How many fathers have that name and ski? Damn few, if not none. Even some of my children's friends with whom they skied in those early years, remember me as "Bonzo ."

Bonzo also came in handy in some other ways. I have a friend, Chuck Jennings, who some years ago was one of the owners of Lite Control Company in Watertown, Massachusetts. Chuck had a very protecting secretary whom he had inherited after his father had retired from the business. Whenever I called his office, the secretary always answered the call and very politely ask "Whom may I say is calling?" I would just as politely respond "Bonzo Serizio ." I could then hear her call in to Chuck's office that there is a "Mr. Serizio on the line for you ." Chuck always took my calls. And, I wonder what went through her mind. Is this Chuck's bookie? He only knows guys with waspy and traditional names like Bill, George, Dick, and Sam.

In later years I have used 'Bonzo" at Starbucks when ordering a Frappiccino because there could be a number of "Chris" there, which has happened to me more than once. I do get a quizzical, fuzzy look from the Barista taking my order and often have to repeat the name, Bonzo. But it works.

Bonzo? Anyway, I have had fun with the name over the years and I think it appropriate to give Bonzo some recognition in this book. So, it really is an autobiography by the author and no ghost writer is actually involved.

Also, my good friend, Titia Bozuwa, cannot be overlooked for recognition. On the weekend of September 8, 2001 Titia ran a writer's workshop at her home in Wakefield, New Hampshire, a beautiful iconic New England town on the Maine border. A dedicated group of writers came to immerse themselves in the fine art of writing and I was one of them. Titia at that time had written two books, *Joan* and *In the Shadow of the Cathedral*. Since then she has written three more, *The Emperor's Guest*, *Wings of Change*, and *Defiance*. I was in the early stages of writing this book and knew I needed help which is why I attended the workshop. However, the inertia and desire to finish my book came to a screeching halt a couple of days later with the horrific 9/11 World Trade Center attacks. I could not get my head back into writing. That Tuesday morning's attack on the United States was a gut wrenching moment for many of Americans and others throughout the world. A lot had changed in a day and it affected me in many ways. One of which is I lost my desire to continue with writing this book.

Tom Strong, my brother-in-law, deserves a lot of credit. He employed his professional craftsmanship and wizardry to do the graphic design work on the front and back covers. Tom is one of those people who kept his childhood playfulness through his adult years and is a very dear friend of mine and many others. Much of the signage at Yale University is some of Tom's creative efforts.

And, most importantly, my financial backers deserve heartwarming recognition and thanks . My sister, Jean Van Curan Pugh, and my daughter, Kristin Van Curan Nordblom, who provided the financing for this random mental autobiographical written journey.

Foreword

Every now and then I reach up to the trap door of the attic of my mind and bring down some recollection of the past. It is fun mostly, sad sometimes, brings joy when necessary to help salve a damaged day. But most importantly the attic is a collection of experiences and thoughts that the author would like to pass on to whoever has the time to read some written words from the past.

I started out my business life in a bank as an auditor, which is like sitting on the tail gate of my truck – always looking backward at the trail of numbers someone else has recorded. It was probably very much like an historian who is always looking backwards as well. But, I soon changed my station in life by leaving the audit department and enjoyed more the looking forward part of life – the working with people, traveling to different places and eager to create and build things.

My mental attic gives me the opportunity to pick and choose anything that's there, in any order, at any time so there is no chronology, no single theme, no messages linked to one another. This is a totally random effort of an old fossil trying to clean out and tidy up his cephalic attic.

Family Background

The following are members of my family some of whom will be mentioned in this book, so I thought it prudent and less confusing to identify them all up front at the beginning.

My father's side of the family – *the Van Curan side*
    My father – *George Lippincott Van Curan (known as "Van")*
    His father – *Christopher James Van Curan*
    His grandfather – *James Van Curen (notice the different spelling)*
    My father's mother – *Edna Lydia Raymond*
    His father's second wife – *Hattie Edith Lippincott – known as "Ede"*
    His father's grandmother – *Elizabeth (maiden name unknown)*
    His father's uncle – *Albert Lippincott – known as "Tip"*
    His father's aunt – *Lulu Lippincott*

My mother's side of the family – *the Dinsmore side*
    My mother – *Juneta Jean Dinsmore (known as "Nettie")*
    Her father – *Regnall Stanford Dinsmore (known as "Reg")*
    Her mother – *Cora Marion Dexter*
    Her grandfather – *Horace Greeley Dinsmore*
    Her mother's grandmother – *Fannie Ellen Towne*
    Her great grandfather – *Ansel Dinsmore*
    Her great grandmother – *Judith Crockett Morse*

My father's side of the family – the Van Curan side.

My father's grandfather, James Van Curen immigrated from Holland in 1848 and settled in Fairport, New York, a small town just outside Rochester. His father, Christopher James Van Curan, owned a hardware store near one of the canals leading to Lake Erie. Unfortunately, Christopher died in 1913 only nine years after my father's birth on March 9, 1904. His mother, Edna, died even sooner in 1909, so George Lippincott Van Curan, my father, really did not get to know either of his parents very well. After his mother died, Christopher married his deceased wife's cousin, Hattie Edith Lippincott, who I had always known as Grandmother Ede. She unfortunately became a widow three years later in 1913 shortly after they were married in 1910. Grandmother Ede then moved in with her sister, Lulu, and brother, Albert (Tip) Lippincott in a house on Woodlawn Avenue in Fairport. She remained a widow the rest of her life which ended in 1956. Neither Lulu nor Tip married. I remember Ede's death because of a small life insurance policy she had from her employment at the American Can Company which provided me with my tuition money in 1956 to enter The Amos Tuck School of Business Administration at Dartmouth College in Hanover, New Hampshire. I think that both Tip and Lulu worked for the American Can Company as well. Ede's job was Secretary to the President and in the "Memorabilia Box" in our house (the contents are identified later at the end of this book), there is a sterling silver engraved velvet lined jewelry box she received as retirement gift from the company. Tip retired early in life with a small pension that enabled him to play golf every day of the summer months and figure skate in the winters at his country club. Tip even taught figure skating at the Club until he was 80.

My father, who was called "Van," grew up under Ede's careful care, loved sports and was a good student, especially in English and Literature. He entered the University of Rochester as a freshman and stayed only for his freshman year. It has been told he played semi-professional baseball for Rochester right after leaving the University, but I have nothing that validates that as a fact. Van then went on to Union College in Schenectady, became a member of Beta Theta Pi fraternity, which was the founding fraternity in the college fraternity movement in United States colleges. He graduated from Union in 1921 and taught freshman English at the University of Rochester for a year. Not satisfied with that as a career start, he chose to become a salesman for the Textbook Division of the Lippincott Publishing Company (Van was no relation to the Lippincott's who owned the company).

His job took him to New York City where in the late 1920's met Juneta Dinsmore, who was working as a buyer for the R. H. Macy department store in the city. They were married in 1931 in a small ceremony and a friend of Juneta's, Carroll ("Inches") Pierce, from Portland, Maine and his wife stood up for them at a private ceremony to get married. Juneta had been married before shortly after high school to Edward French of Norway, Maine, her hometown. But, that marriage was annulled shortly after it took place because Edward French was an alcoholic. Juneta kept that fact from my sister, Jean, and me for many years and I suspect it was a non-event in her life and did not want to ever discuss it.

My mother's side of the family – the Dinsmore side.
Regnall Stanford Dinsmore, my grandfather, was born on July 18, 1886 in the family farmhouse as had his father, Horace Greely Dinsmore. The farmhouse was built by my great-great grandfather, Ansel Dinsmore, in 1839. The Dinsmore farm remains on what is called "Round the Pond" Road at the head of Fire Lane 18 or Sandy Shore Lane on the east side of Lake Penneseewassee in Norway, Maine. Reg's father was a farmer and a carpenter as was his father. Reg followed in his father's and grandfather's footsteps. Reg also had a great love of the outdoors and for writing about it. In the 1920's, 30's and early 40's

he wrote articles for *Fur, Fish & Game*, *Redbook*, and *Blue Book*, which were popular pulp magazines then. Reg tried his hand at radio scripts with the help of his cousin, Victor Whitman, who also lived in Norway. When radio became popular in the mid-1930's *Young Widder Brown*, *Mary Back Stage Wife*, and the *Cisco Kid* were scripts he had a hand in writing. Reg's dream was to have a story published by *The Saturday Evening Post*, but it never came to reality even though every script he wrote was first submitted to them and returned by them.

Cora Marion Dexter, my grandmother, was born in Auburn, Maine in 1887 and brought up in West Paris, Maine. Both Reg and Cora were 1904 graduates of Norway High School. Juneta Jean Dinsmore, my mother, was the oldest of their three children to be followed by Olive and Stan. In 1911 with three young children Cora took all three kids across the country by train to San Diego to meet up with Reg who had preceded her there to find carpentry work. They only stayed a little over a year and returned to Norway to live again on the Dinsmore farm.

My mother, Juneta, also known as "Nettie," was born on December 29, 1907 in Greenville, Maine and graduated from Norway (ME) High School in 1921. She was the salutatorian of her class. Someone who had recently moved to town was the valedictorian much to the ire of many townspeople, including Juneta. After high school she went to Boston University for two years and then on to New York City. Juneta was as kind and loving mother as you could ever have. She smoked Camel cigarettes most of her adult life and it caught up to her later as she succumbed to emphysema and died in June 1990 at the Stephens Memorial Hospital in Norway, Maine.

Your author, Christopher Dexter Van Curan, was born on July 19, 1932 at the Wickersham Hospital on East 53th Street in New York City. The hospital is no longer there as it was torn down and replaced later by seedy businesses, such as the Pussy Cat Lounge, only to be replaced again by CitiBank. That historic fact may explain why I went into banking for much of my life. I escaped the earlier clutch which may have led me to manage scruffy lounges. Three weeks after I was born, my father had to make a difficult choice of whether to work half days at half pay for the Lippincott Publishing Company or take the next six months off as a leave of absence. The Great Depression was in full force and the choice was easy. Van moved the family to Norway, Maine and we lived with Juneta's parents, Reg and Cora Dinsmore. I wish that Lippincott Publishing had made their offer to Van earlier so that I could have been born in Maine. As it is, I shall always be "from away" and cannot claim to be a native "Mainer ." I am a native "New Yorker," which doesn't do much for me. I think they lived in town that winter even though the Dinsmore family farmhouse was on Crockett Ridge in Norway.

On December 28, 1933 Jean Lippincott Van Curan, my sister, was born in Grove City, Pennsylvania in the University Hospital. The temperature that day was 13 below zero according to my grandmother Cora's diary. We were living in Grove City because Van had landed a sales job for The Macmillan Publishing Company. Jean graduated from White Plains (NY) High School in 1951, went to Colby College, and married a Colby classmate, Larry Pugh, who was a class behind her. Larry had grown up with us in White Plains but had gone away to the Salisbury School, a Connecticut prep school before college. Jean was married to Larry for 59 years before his passing in December 2016, raised two wonderful daughters, has four grandsons and a great granddaughter. Larry was a retired Fortune 100 company Chairman and CEO of VF Corporation (owning brand names like Lee, Wrangler, JanSport, North Face, and Vanity Fair lingerie) and was very active in civic and cultural affairs on a local and national level. Both Jean and Larry received doctorates from Colby a few years ago to recognize their dedicated service to the college where the international studies building bears their names on the

Colby campus. Jean is also a sister every brother wishes to have. I have enjoyed her kindness and generosity for these many years I have been on this side of the grass.

My dad, Van, died on May 1, 1954 in Norway after having suffered two previous heart attacks. As a boy he had what was later suspected as rheumatic fever which had weakened his heart. He had retired from The Macmillan Company only a month before and had retirement plans to build a house on Round the Pond road on the 38 acres he had bought in 1946. The land had a quarter of a mile of shore front and the sale of the shore front lots paid my sister's and my college tuitions – Jean at Colby College and me at Middlebury College. These shore lots in the mid-1950's sold for $75 a foot of lakefront footage and two lots of 75 feet each would pay for one year of college for the two of us. Thirty years later in the 1980's the shore lots on the east side of the lake were being sold for $1000 a foot and got assessed that way as well.

I graduated from Middlebury College in Vermont in 1954, a month and a half after my dad's death. Less than a week later, I married Betsy Strong, also a Middlebury graduate a class ahead of me, who grew up in Hanover, New Hampshire. Graduation and the wedding were bitter sweet for me. Dad was not there to celebrate either event with me. Betsy and I lived in Middlebury for the summer and in October I entered the US Army which took me to Fort Dix, New Jersey for basic training. I had volunteered for the military since I had a very low Selective Service number and knew I would be drafted into the service shortly after graduation. Part of the reasoning to volunteer was to get into the service to gain the benefits of active service during the Korean War. After 8 weeks of basic training I got assigned to Headquarters Company, United States Army, Fort Myer, Virginia as a clerk typist. I was a Private E-2, lowest of the low in the ranks of the US Army. But, I had a very rewarding military service experience. I wound up in G-2 Intelligence working for the Central Intelligence Agency and the National Indications Center, a super-secret intelligence collection center located in the sub-basement of the Pentagon. We briefed the Joint Chiefs of Staff on military and political intelligence around the world every Wednesday morning. Fascinating work and highly, highly secret. I had what was known as a Top Secret-Code Word security clearance. The code word back then was "Eider."

My children:

Ann, my oldest daughter, was born on April 11, 1955 at Fort Belvoir, Virginia. We initially lived in an apartment on Glebe Road in Alexandria, but a few months later got flooded out. That flooding motivated us to move up stream to Arlington Mill Drive in Arlington and also a little closer my work at the Pentagon. Annie lives in Calgary, Alberta, Canada and is married to Dr. Kevin Johnson, an emergency room physician. They met at Dartmouth College and both were the Class of 1977. Annie was on the Dartmouth Ski Team and Kevin was on the Dartmouth Hockey team. They have three boys; Peter, Nick and Ben. All three are married to sweethearts who have produced three beautiful great granddaughters with two more on the way. Peter works for Fluor in Farnham, England. He and Julia have two daughters, Evie and Greer, plus a boy on the way in January, 2018. Nick is married to Teresa and they live in Edmonton, Alberta, Canada with one daughter, Mila, with another on the way in November, 2017. Nick just finished playing in the professional National Hockey League and Swedish Hockey League after graduating from Dartmouth in 2008. Ben is married to Danielle and they jointly run a graphic design firm in Vancouver, British Columbia, Canada.

Darby, whose name came from Darby Field, the first ascendant of Mt. Washington, was born on December 8, 1956 in Hanover, New Hampshire and tragically died four months later in March from sudden infant death syndrome. Darby is buried next to her grandfather, Robert Chamberlain Strong, and her grandmother, Dorothy Morgan Strong, in the Hanover cemetery just south of Hanover. Darby's grave stone puts her in great Dartmouth company as in a nearby plot are Ernest Martin Hopkins and John Sloane Dickey, both long time revered Dartmouth College presidents.

Dirk was also born in Hanover on February 20, 1958 during a very snowy winter by Dr. Boardman, who had also delivered Darby. The snow banks were so high you could not see other cars at the street intersections. Yellow tennis balls mounted on top of car antennas alerted drivers at intersections that another car was there as well. The icicles from our second floor apartment roof, which was an old Army barracks at 200 Wigwam Circle, connected to the ground below. Dirk's name came from Edna Ferber's book, "So Big ." Dirk is the IT Director for the Greely schools in Cumberland, Maine where he lives with his partner, Michelle. Dirk has two boys, Dirk II and Tanner plus a daughter, Greta. Dirk II works for Sysco in Seattle, Washington. Tanner is attending the University of Southern Maine in Portland and working for Whole Foods there in Portland. Greta is finishing up her senior year at Greely High School in Cumberland, Maine and looking at colleges to attend. Dirk spent a good deal of his early adulthood in the Vail Valley of Colorado representing ski companies, managing a high end management retreat center for American Express, and ski racing when he could. When he was working for American Express, he managed their hospitality suite at the U. S. Tennis Open in Flushing, New York for 15 years.

Kristin was born in Waltham, Massachusetts on June 4, 1960 at the Newton Wellesley Hospital. Kristin was the most expensive of the four children. Ann cost $7 because the US Army only charged $1 a day for the mother's meals in the Army hospital. She was definitely worth it. Kris, as she likes to be called, is married to Peter Nordblom, who manages his family real estate development business in Burlington, Massachusetts. They have three boys (Todd, Anders and Crosby), two of whom are married. Todd, who works for his father, is married to Amy and have one daughter, Lucy. Crosby was recently married to Greta and live in Seattle as does his older brother, Anders, who works for REI.

After graduating from The Amos Tuck School in June 1958 I took an entry level position with The First National Bank of Boston for $5,500 a year and spent 29 years there in various positions. When I took an early retirement in 1987 I was a Division Executive for the Insurance Banking Group and earning $86,000. I then went into the insurance business for a few years and consulting for a few more after that. Along the way I was a founder of four businesses; The Arbor Group (insurance), Wildcat Academy (education), and Lincoln Canoe Company (manufacturing) and Van Curan & Associates (consulting). This entrepreneurial passion still exists and currently I have shared it with undergraduate and graduate students at Endicott College as well as Salem State University, where I have been a member of the faculty. I am also on the faculty at the New England School of Acupuncture in Newton, Massachusetts where I teach the Practice Development courses there. Plus, I do some consulting and mentoring for business owners and managers who want to accomplish their vision and mission for their business. One of my clients is the Executive Service Corps, a nonprofit consulting firm which only works with other nonprofits in northern New England. I have been associated with the ESC since 1996 and for many years did volunteer consulting for them in the Boston area, Maine, New Hampshire and Vermont.

After 26 years of marriage, Betsy and I divorced. I was 48 and probably going through a mid-life crisis. Two years after my divorce, I married Sandra (Sandy) Lynne Marx in a small country ceremony at the Norway Center Church and we have been married for 35 years. Sandy was a flight attendant for Overseas National Airways (ONA) when I met her. She came to Boston to be the Functions Manager for the Harvard Club in Boston and later for two Boston hotels. Currently she is special services ground staff for British Airways (BA) at Logan Airport in Boston and has been there for over 19 years. It is a demanding job on the front line dealing with passengers all day and she has enough stories to write at least three books on her experiences with the airlines and her passengers. One book would be on her ONA trips around the world as a charter airline flight attendant, another on evacuating Viet Nam infant orphans from Saigon, and another on her experiences at BA over 19+ years.

Shortly after Sandy met my mother, Nettie, we were having drinks one evening before supper (supper in Maine is the evening meal and dinner is lunch, just in case you didn't know). Nettie had kept her airline swizzle stick when she flew with friends to Hawaii via Las Vegas. It was an ONA swizzle stick so it is quite possible that Nettie had been on one of Sandy's flights in the mid-1970's.

My greatest pride is having eight wonderful grandsons and then a beautiful gifted granddaughter. They in turn have produced four great granddaughters with two more great grandchildren on the way.

1. Peter Johnson
2. Nick Johnson
3. Ben Johnson
4. Todd Nordblom
5. Anders Nordblom
6. Crosby Nordblom
7. Dirk Van Curan II
8. Tanner Van Curan
9. Greta Van Curan

They are all special in their own way and are carving out meaningful lives.

As I turned 85 in July 2017 I have been truly blessed with the life I have lived. The friendships I have formed, both business and personal, the family bonds with Jean's family, the things I have done, the experiences I have had, the places I have been, and the love I have shared with family and friends is precious. I am hopeful it will last at least another ten years or so, if my health holds out. I tell people "I am in good shape for the shape I'm in ." Boston's Cardinal Cushing used that phrase and I have borrowed it.

But, enough about me. Let's get into the attic for some stories which I hope do not bore you.

Van Curan family with Van, Chris, and Juneta

Jean and Chris

Chris, Betsy, Dirk, Annie, and Kristin at Old Speck Mountain

Annie, Dirk, and Kristin

Juneta

Painting of Juneta by Vivian Akers

View of Tuckerman Ravine from HoJo

Reg with his model canoe

Reg and Cora Dinsmore's 50th Wedding Anniversary

Chris as a Private First Class in US Army at the Pentagon

Chris at his 25th Tuck School Reunion

Sandy at Chris' 25th Tuck School Reunion

Chris and Jean

Chris' 8 and Jean's 4 grandsons on our deck in Maine

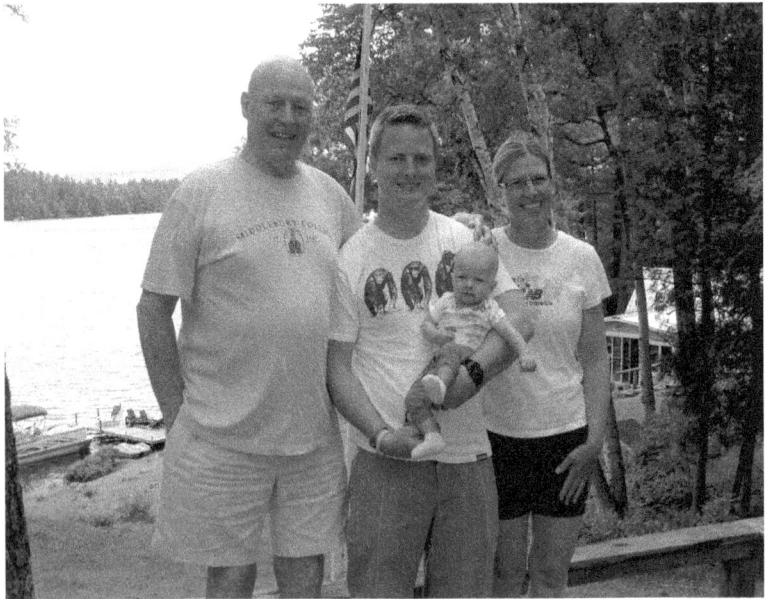

4 generations with the Johnsons

Wildcat Mountain

This is a story about a downhill ski race at Wildcat Mountain in New Hampshire, the Mount Washington Observatory, and Al Risch with a Tucker SnoCat.

As I said this book is in random order. Why did I start with a Wildcat Mountain story and this little vignette? No reason. I love the mountains and you might say I am a mountain tropic person and especially a White Mountain tropic person. I worked for the Appalachian Mountain Club and the U. S. Forest Service at Dolly Copp Campground in the White Mountain National Forest which is only a few miles north of Wildcat on NH Route 16. Those were truly enjoyable summers in the mountains. Then too, the winters that I spent at Wildcat seeing three great kids, Annie, Dirk and Kristin, develop into young adults coupled with the parental pride that came from working with the Wildcat Junior ski racing program are great pleasures for a father. I also served on the Wildcat Mountain Corporation Board of Directors for about 10 years.

Downhill races in the East for junior ski racers were almost non-existent and yet downhills are a very important part of a young ski racers development. Many ski areas were hosting slalom and giant slalom races, but most areas did not have the terrain, the ski area management support or the ski club support or the "guts" to host a downhill race. Wildcat was fortunate that it had all four plus Wildcat directors had strong alpine racing backgrounds. Bookie Dodge, George Macomber and Malcolm McLane were all Olympic skiers and on the Wildcat Board of Directors. The fifth ingredient was having a professional ski patrol director, Al Risch, very interested in these kids and downhill racing. Downhill is probably the most difficult race to organize and manage. It takes three days of dedicating a race trail and three days of on-trail personnel to manage all the logistics and safety, not to mention all the race officiating that has to be in place all three days.

What shouldn't take place at any race is some out-of-bounds racers throwing cement blocks out of gondola windows onto public ski trails below them and then having their coach, Bud Burgess from Pittsfield, Massachusetts defending those young ski racer's rights after they are caught by the mountain management, to compete in the race. They were disqualified at Wildcat, but managed to race later at Mt. Cranmore by their misguided coach.

Al Risch made sure the Wildcat downhill trail was in excellent condition and that all the safety nets, hay bales, and crossing barriers were in place. In return for all his work, Al only wanted to be the first forerunner in each of the downhills put on at Wildcat.

One of those races was etched into the chemical portion of my memory. I think this chemical memory is permanent storage area. The electrical memory is the more recent memory awaiting permanent storage. Malcolm McLane, was a perennial starter at most Wildcat races and I was often his alternate at the start. Sometimes we traded roles. Malcolm was Chairman of the Wildcat Mountain Corporation Board, one of the original investors and had a long history of ski racing as well as having children in the racing program.

It was one of those typical cold, windy days at Wildcat on the nose of the start of the course above the section known as "Sun

Valley" and the old "S" turns of the old Wildcat racing trail. Al had arranged to have one of the old Tucker Snowcats parked above the start so that we could keep all our gear in the back and, at the break between the two runs, have a chance to warm up in the cab. The Snowcat idled throughout the day with the heater on full blast and was a welcome sanctuary for the start officials. We had a large field of racers and at the completion of the second run it was beginning to get cloudy with ugly weather racing in from the West across the summit of Mt. Washington. The post runner had finished his run and the course personnel had taken down the fifteen gates to the finish line for us to pick up in the Snowcat when we came down. Malcolm left the start area at the completion of the race and I had volunteered to dismantle the starting and communication equipment, shovel out the start area so it would not be a skier risk and piled all the equipment into the back of the Snowcat. Al arrived as it was getting darker to drive the Snowcat down the mountain to the maintenance garage and drop off the race equipment at the Den, the Ski Club's headquarters. I decided that was the better way off the mountain that day and I was not enjoying the cold blasts coming straight in across Pinkham Notch. Al climbed into the cab, tromped on the accelerator and the machine coughed, sputtered and died. When Al turned the ignition key – NOTHING. DEAD. The fan belt had been slipping all day and the battery was dead.

You just don't jump start a Snowcat on the downhill pitch of the Wildcat trail and if you do, you stand a good chance of quickly ending up in Berlin, New Hampshire some 25 miles away as the crow flies or even Montreal, which is the route we could be taking. With the battery dead, we had no mountain management communications with the mountain's maintenance garage and no easy way of getting off the mountain which was now in total darkness. All of the ski patrol had done their mountain trail "sweeps," which assures the patrol that there is no skier left on any trail, and the patrolmen had left the patrol's first aid building for the day so no one was monitoring the ski patrol radios. Al's radio was not to be heard at Wildcat for the rest of the day. He decided to keep switching channels with a hope that someone would be monitoring one of the channels somewhere, otherwise we would be walking down the mountain leaving the dead Snowcat there until the night snow groomers came on their shift to work on the trails and could get it started.

By some stroke of good luck we finally got a response from the Mt. Washington Observatory who picked up our call on one of their many radios. They made a telephone call to the Wildcat maintenance garage and we got another Snowcat up to the mountain to take us off. There was no life threating issue here at all, but you get to really respect the weather and the mountain. We had plenty of clothing to stay warm and we were out of the wind while we waited. We could have walked down as well without any great risk.

July 4th on the Wilbur Cross Parkway

I learned to drive a year before I was sixteen years old when my uncle, Sam Chandler, would let me drive his World War II Jeep during the summer on the dirt roads on Goat Island where he lived and my parents had their summer camp on Lake Penneseewassee in Norway, Maine. This was just after World War II and he had recently returned from having been in the Military Air Transport Command ferrying B-24's to Russia. As an aside, Uncle Sam graduated in the early 1920s from the University of Maine and after graduation went into flying the U. S. Mail from Portland to Bangor to Boston. He had one of the first commercial pilots licenses in the United States. He was also the first pilot to land a commercial aircraft at the new Auburn – Lewiston International Airport.

I never took a driver education course at White Plains (NY) High School because I thought I knew it all and back then in 1948 there was no driver education insurance discount incentive to take the course. I don't recall taking the exam or the road test, but I must have passed it. I can usually parallel park my 2013 Ford F-150 truck with ease so I must have learned something.

My real driving lesson came on July 4, 1948. Our family would always try to get to our summer camp in Maine from White

Plains, New York for the Fourth of July. The family got up early that morning to get a good start which took us up the Merritt and Wilber Cross Parkways in Connecticut. We were all in the car that 1948 summer morning and I was at the wheel of our 1939 Chevy sedan that had a vacuum shift as I recall. When no one was looking or that attentive I would shift into the next highest gear by letting up on the accelerator and move the gear shift into the higher gear. No problem.

That early July morning was becoming bright with a clear blue sky, dry roads and would have been a beautiful day. However.

Black smoke began to appear on the horizon not far ahead of us and as we drove further, the smoke got darker, denser and higher in the sky near North Haven, Connecticut. We were about the sixth car to come upon the most grizzly accident scene I had ever encountered in my young life. Two young couples about my age in an Oldsmobile convertible had hit the right side of the bridge abutment as they attempted to make a curve in the highway under the cement overpass. The Oldsmobile convertible had tipped over on its top with three of the four people trapped underneath the burning car. The fourth was thrown out of the car about 100 yards up the road dressed in a stripped T-shirt covered in blood and dying. One of the earlier arriving drivers was trying to attend to the only survivor they could get to. The fire and heat were so intense there was nothing that could be done to get the three trapped passengers out of the burning convertible. When, after the New Haven Fire Department had put out the fire and the tow truck tipped over the smoky convertible, the three charred and very dead bodies fell out on to the steaming, smoking highway. Death at its ugliest and an indelible mental image lasting for life.

When Dad asked me if I wanted to continue on driving after the road had been cleared, I declined as my stomach for driving was in a severe state of shock and sorrow. That vivid, horrible memory has stayed with me for years and has probably contributed to my pretty good driving record over the years. Well, maybe. I did hit a lawyer on a bicycle in 1968 with my '57 VW bug later. This story to be told later.

And, some twenty years later I bought a 1966 Ford Mustang black convertible. Also, my wife, Sandy, had a 1961 VW Super Beetle ivory white convertible. My feelings for convertibles must have improved considerably over those intervening years.

Thanksgiving Turkey Caper at Bank of Boston

The Wednesday before Thanksgiving is usually a non-eventful day in the banking world. The lending platform officers have arranged their travel schedules to be either home or to be calling in the morning on some customer that is in the same town as their grandparents who have invited the family for the holiday. At around 2PM the third floor at the Bank of Boston was sparsely populated with only the more diligent loan officer or the officer who was single with no Thanksgiving plans. Bill Brown, the President, was about to make his annual Wednesday pre-Thanksgiving stroll around the lending floors to take inventory of the stalwart officers still struggling it out at their desks. This strolling event is his one and only of the year and you could count on it.

Downstairs on the second floor where all the chief executives are housed, there were the usual heady meetings taking place on some lofty subject like budgets, loan loss reserve provisions or retail banking strategy. Also on the second floor were housed at the other end of the building were the Special Industries loan officers who did all the big movie and entertainment loans. These people were the kind of elite of the commercial bankers trained in the Serge Semenenko methodologies, who was a legendary banking figure.

It was on those two floors in the mid- 1970's that one pre-Thanksgiving became a comedy. It could become a Broadway play as it played out during the day before Thanksgiving and into the early pre-Thanksgiving evening.

Bob Mahoney, a rising young banker, started the "play' into motion on that Wednesday morning when he received a call from one of his customers. As a Thanksgiving gift the customer offered to deliver some scallops which he knew Bob loved because he did not like turkey. The customer would have them delivered later in the day. When they were delivered, Bob was at lunch and his caring secretary took the unmarked bag of scallops down to the second floor Executive Conference Room kitchen. She put them in the refrigerator to hold until Bob left for the holiday.

Meanwhile, Dot Claussen, the Chairman's secretary who resided on the second floor adjacent to the Executive Conference Room and Chairman Dick Hill's office, went out to a late lunch to pick up a fresh dressed turkey in the Faneuil Hall marketplace. She had ordered her turkey earlier in the month. She planned on preparing Thanksgiving dinner for herself and her aging mother in Somerville where they both lived. Upon her return from lunch she placed the bagged turkey into the Executive Conference Room refrigerator where it resided the remainder of the day – just in front of the bagged scallops which Bob Mahoney's secretary had put there earlier.

In mid-afternoon Bob Mahoney left the bank early to avoid the rush of holiday traffic. He picked up his bag of scallops from the front top shelf of the refrigerator in a hurried state and left the Bank.

Shortly afterwards, Dick Hill had told Dot that she could leave early and the only thing of importance that afternoon was a meeting scheduled with Bill Brown, President, and Eugene Tangney, Executive Vice President, which would be in his office. He had nothing for her that necessitated keeping her around all afternoon. Gratefully, Dot meticulously put all her files away, locked up the file cabinets, straightened up her desk, went to the closet to get her coat and then proceeded to the refrigerator to get her turkey out and head home on the MBTA rapid transit line to Somerville.

The meeting Dick Hill had scheduled was already in progress as Dot approached the refrigerator to find her turkey was missing. The only other thing in the refrigerator was an unmarked bag bearing no resemblance to the bag which she had placed there only a couple of hours earlier.

A very distraught and tearful eyed Chairman's secretary went back to her desk with her coat on. Dick Hill noticed her return, got up from his meeting and asked her whether there was a problem. "Someone stole my turkey" was her response.

The second floor of The First National Bank of Boston at 100 Federal Street had guarded entrances, patrolling security officers and very few occupants. The spiral staircase leading from the third floor to the second floor also has a security activated lock which was used frequently by the loan officers on the third floor to access the top brass. Yet with all that security someone had walked off with Dot's Thanksgiving turkey.

Dick Hill's meeting immediately got an unscheduled agenda item - help Dot find the turkey and apprehend the culprit who stole it. The guards were quickly alerted and some very high level planning started to take place. The kind of planning that was never before contemplated in the Chairman's office.

As their lofty plans were being assembled, one of the elite lenders, Tom Bubier of the Special Industries Group, was leaving as well a "little" early to get home to his family. One of his customers had sent him a turkey which was delivered to his desk. His turkey was in a box which he had under his arm as he made his way to the elevators past the security guards who had been fully alerted to the "turkey robbery ." Spying the turkey, the on-duty guard intercepted Tom and marched him into the Chairman's office thinking the mystery had been solved.

Dot, still quite distraught, was asked to identify the turkey and immediately told the guards, Dick Hill, Bill Brown and Gene Tangney that this was not her turkey as hers was in a bag. Not in a box. Tom, who was irritated at not being able to leave as planned and being charged with theft was vindicated by Dot's information and was then free to leave.

The turkey theft and helping Dot get a replacement turkey were getting some expert executive attention. Gene mentioned that he had a call earlier from his wife, Mary, who said that not all their family guests were able to make it to their Wellesley home for Thanksgiving for which she had bought two turkeys. Now, she needed only one for the smaller gathering. Bill Brown suggested that since he lived in Weston, adjacent to Wellesley, that his chauffeur after leaving him off at his home could drive to Gene's house to pick up the second turkey. The chauffer could then drive the turkey to Dot's house in Somerville and could be there by 6 PM. Thus, the problem of getting a turkey for Dot's Thanksgiving was solved.

A very high level management group had had a very unique personnel problem and were able to solve it with dispatch and a personally chauffeur delivered turkey to one of the Bank's key staff members. The in-house newspaper never picked up on the story and until now it has never been reduced to writing. But, it doesn't quite end there, which is what you might expect.

In the early evening in the Marblehead home of Dick and Polly Hill, which is on Marblehead Neck, a telephone call arrived. Polly answered it and told Dick that Bob Mahoney was on the phone and could he come to the phone. Bob explained that he had picked up a bag in the refrigerator when he left the Bank that afternoon and expected the bag he took were the scallops which his secretary had placed there. Much to his surprise when he got home a few minutes ago to find his scallops were instead a turkey which had a tag with Dot Claussen's name on it. Bob said "I think I've got a problem ." To which Dick said "Your damned right you have a problem ." Bob explained that he didn't like turkey, which is why he accepted the scallops. This was not the problem which Dick had expected from this young loan officer. Dick's final retort was "This Thanksgiving you are going to like turkey ."

The following year a few things had changed. Bob Mahoney was given an assignment in the Bank's London office. This was not punishment, but recognition that Bob had a bright future with the Bank and it was a "grooming" station for more responsibility. Security got beefed up on the executive floor. Dot became more cautious about storing precious items in the refrigerator.

That following year I recalled the turkey robbery caper of the year before and decided to have a little more fun with the event. I sent a London Office telex to Bob on the Wednesday before Thanksgiving which said "Thank you, Bob. No one stole my turkey this year." Signed: Dot Klosson (purposely misspelled).

Reg Dinsmore at the Oxford County Fair

This event happened around September 1942 at the old Oxford County Fair Grounds where the Oxford Hills Comprehensive High School now resides. It was a big plot of land with a race track for the trotters and a baseball diamond. There was a big exhibit hall to house all the craft and farm produce on display for prizes. The trotters and their sulkies came for the week to race and were great fun to watch. Two dollar bills were much in evidence at the betting windows. The annual old timers baseball game between Norway and South Paris was always well attended. The twin towns as they are called had a bitter rivalry going as a number of the old timers had gone to their respective high schools in their town so the rivalry goes back to their high school days. Today that rivalry doesn't exist since the regional school system consolidated these two towns along with a number of others in the area.

Bill Young, who was a turkey farmer on Crockett Ridge in Norway, was the pitcher for the Norway town team. Bill was a wiry agile fellow. Not very tall, but could pitch a pretty mean fast ball at 55 years old. My grandfather, Reg Dinsmore, was the catcher and also lived on Crockett Ridge. Bill and Reg had grown up together on their farms on the Ridge. When Reg needed ice to stock his ice house, he would call on Bill to use his two gigantic oxen to twitch and haul the ice from the lake to the ice house up behind Reg and Cora's log cabin alongside the lake. There they would pack the blocks of ice in sawdust in layer upon layer and it would last until almost August depending on the early summer temperatures. The two of them were a team.

Cora, my sister Jean, and I were sitting in the grandstands near home plate watching the big game. I think Norway was ahead by a run. It was South Paris' turn at bat in the bottom of the ninth inning.

Between the grandstands and home plate was a fence, much like a snow fence to keep the wild pitches and foul balls from going all the way back to the grandstands. The fence played an important role often during those games and during the Fair. During the trotter races, it kept the horses from going into the infield and during the ball games, kept the baseball within the infield. One of Bill's pitches was hit by a South Paris batter and it was fouled up and back towards the grandstand. Reg threw off his catcher's mask and ran back to catch the ball which was just beyond the retaining fence. He leaped over the fence, caught the seat of his pants on the fence, ripped a wide tear in them and caught the ball for the out and retired the side to win the game. The Norway half the crowd went wild and the South Paris half went dead silent. The Norway team was victorious. If Reg had to play another inning, he might have been charged with indecent exposure and if there ever was any underwear question about briefs? Or shorts? Definitely shorts. Cora was mortified. Jean and I got a good laugh from it.

Grandmother Cora Playing Rummy

When Cora Dexter was a young girl growing up in West Paris in the Inn which her parents operated near the railroad station, she accidently burned the palm of her right hand on a hot woodstove in the kitchen. That accident seared her hand so badly that it could not be opened all the way. She went through life with this crippled hand this way without complaint.

She was an amazing woman as she never let that deformity keep her from cooking great meals for crowds of people, or firing a shotgun in some woodcock cover in Hebron or trout fishing at Upper Dam on Richardson Lake. And, there was always the "regulation" cake which was always in my grandfather's lunch box every day when he went off to work on a carpentry job. Regulation cake is a delicious spice cake with chocolate frosting twice the thickness of the cake.

The first time I really became aware of her inability to do something with her hands was when we played Rummy, a card game. She could not shuffle playing cards. When it got to be her turn to shuffle, she would have either Jean or me do it for her. But, she insisted in dealing out the cards.

She could tie a fly on a leader. She could stir a pot of beans. She could drive a car. She could do almost everything but shuffle playing cards.

Lost Room at the Pentagon

I was drafted into the US Army on October 8, 1954 and the Korean War was still a conflict. My Selective Service Board in White Plains, New York which is where I had to register for the draft at age 18, told me my draft number was very low and I would no doubt be drafted within a couple of months after graduation from Middlebury College. It made no sense to me to go on to graduate school and even though I had been recently married, my being drafted was virtually assured.

As a geography – geology major at Middlebury, I had a fellow fraternity brother who also had the same major and graduated two years ahead of me. He was in the US Army using his geography major skills with a Strategic Intelligence Team (G-2) at the Pentagon in Washington, DC. He had written me and suggested that I replace him on that team when he got out of the service in the fall of 1954. I wrote him back to accept the offer and to get instructions as to how to engineer such an event.

My instructions were to write Sargent Welchel, Headquarters Company, US Army, Fort Myer, Virginia immediately upon my entrance into the service. I should give him all the background about my fraternity brother's G-2 assignment, my geography major background including my cartography courses I had in college and most important my serial number with my service unit address in Fort Dix, New Jersey when I got there for 8 weeks of basic training boot camp. I did all that with great haste upon my arrival at Fort Dix.

My letter never received a response. I thought it had probably gone into one of those dark Pentagon closets never to be heard from again. Meanwhile most of the graduating basic training classes at Fort Dix were going to Korea or Germany, which was a looming possibility for me as the eight weeks went on.

My answer came at the beginning of the eighth week as the assignments are read out by the base full bird Colonel at an assembly of all the graduating classes. Of course, I had the usual wait to hear everyone else's assignment – at least those with last names "A's" through to the "U's ." They were mostly going to Korea and a very few with specialties were going to West Germany. My name finally came up in the alphabet order. "Christopher Dexter Van Curan. Assigned to Headquarters Company, Fort Myer, Virginia ." The Colonel paused. He read the assignment again. Same as before. Paused again. Then he said "Sounds like a tour of duty in Arlington, VA at the Tomb of the Unknown Soldier ." My heart sank. But, I hoped for the best.

The rest of that week the training cadre in my training squad, many of my fellow soldiers, and including myself, were mystified at my assignment. Usually the Tomb of the Unknown Soldier assignments goes to someone with a lot of political clout or has a family with a strong military background, or someone who has distinguished themselves in the military. You are committed to drinking no alcohol during your service time and have to pledge a total 24/7/365 commitment to serving the unknown soldier. None of those fit me for sure. The hardnosed training cadre however backed off on me for the rest of the week with all their harassment techniques since I was something of an oddity. Hell, I could have told them that even without this assignment.

On to Washington, DC and Headquarters Company. I had

never seen more Master Sergeants anywhere in my life. Generals, Colonels, Majors were all over the place. What I found out was that the Headquarters Company not only had a duty to protect and honor the Tomb of the Unknown Soldier, but was also the support unit for all the Army personnel stationed at the Pentagon. The Master Sergeants were US Army Reserve Colonels and Majors, many of whom had field commissions, who had to give those ranks up when the military had a reduction in force (hence the term "riffed"). These guys were filling out their 20 years to get their pension at the higher officer levels.

I never saw Sargent Welchel, the benefactor in getting my assignment. In fact, when I arrived I found that the G-2 Strategic Intelligence Teams had been disbanded. Fortunately that event occurred after I left Fort Dix and before I arrived at Fort Myer. My Commanding Officer however had cut some orders for me to join another G-2 intelligence group being formed called "The National Indications Center (NIC) to be located in the sub-basement of the Pentagon.

My security clearances had to be obtained. I would need every clearance that existed, but one, a "Crypto" clearance. I was to be cleared up through Code Word Top Secret. Fortunately all my references were in the First Military District. The Army Security Agency called on every one I had listed and many more as well. It was a three month process. A fellow service member, Charlie Kellogg, who arrived with me was vying for the same slot, which I found out later his father was the Secretary of Commerce and Agriculture (in other words "clout"). Charlie's references spanned two military districts, which took longer to process, and in the end I won the race for the position as the lowest ranking serviceman in the NIC.

While the First Military District's ASA boys were investigating my background to determine my suitability to hold some of the nation's deepest secrets, I was temporarily assigned to the US Army Attaché Property Unit in the Pentagon. My superior was a

Chief Warrant Officer from the South who amazingly assigned me to a desk whose last occupant was named "Van Keuren ." I never found out where that Van Keuren went and there was never any lingering correspondence that would lead me to him.

My job was to package up shipments of all kinds of things for the Army Attaches located around the world. We had a small supply room in the Pentagon which had a red seal on the door to indicate a special restricted top secret access. The shipments were varied. We sent out Minox cameras with the newly created black and white Tri-X high speed film developed by Kodak and tested secretly at the McCarthy Senate hearings to see if inside low light photographs could become useful in intelligence gathering. We also sent out miniphones with small highly sensitive microphones clipped to the inside of one's shirt to secretly record conversations. We also sent out expensive Leica cameras with all the accessories including telephoto lenses. Some of my compatriots purposely "lost" their cameras and had to pay the replacement cost. I think the ridiculous replacement cost was like $50 for some $500 worth of equipment. The stupid kind of things that were shipped out were the recent Book of the Month Club selections and Readers Digest, etc.

One day the key to this red seal designated room was again entrusted to me to package up the orders received from the overseas Attaché offices. I spent a good part of the day in this totally enclosed room with no windows on the fifth floor, D ring of the "Puzzle Palace," as the Pentagon is sometimes referred to by its inhabitants. My mistake at the end of the day was I had locked the door behind me and left the key on the inside of the now locked room. It was a very embarrassed Private E-2 who informed the Chief Warrant Officer that the key was locked on the inside of the supply room. "No Problem" he replies since the Pentagon guards had a duplicate key to every Pentagon room in their command center in the sub-basement. We both proceeded down to their command center and requested one of the officers to obtain the duplicate key. We went to the big board in another room where indeed there were thousands of keys all labeled with their respective doors. We checked the 5D row of keys and went to the room number, which was something like 246. But, there was no 246 room key and no room 246 on the board. The officer then accompanied us up to the room 5D246 and found it really existed. A little mystified we all returned to the command center and got out the floor plan diagrams which were much like engineers drawings for each of the floors. There was no 5D246!!!! Therefore, no key.

The security officer called on one of the civilian dressed Army Security Agents, who was in the office and a reputed expert lock picker to go back up with me to pick the lock and get the key locked on the inside. My CWO went back to his office and the Pentagon security officer returned to his other duties.

There we were the two of us, the civilian dressed ASA agent and me dressed in military cloth with a Private E-2 patch on my sleeves picking a Corbin lock of a red seal secret room door in the Pentagon without being challenged by any one – security guards, other military or anyone. The ASA agent finally succeeded after an hour of frustrations with the complicated lock system and I got to retrieve the precious key.

There is now a duplicate key for Room 5D246 in the Pentagon. And, the security officer drew in the missing room on his floor drawings.

Winter Bumper Riding

This is a story which no mother and probably no father as well will want their child to read. It is not intended to be a lesson book on how to ride bumpers on snowy roads. Today the way most modern cars are constructed, it would be very difficult to grab on to a bumper. So this story should not be a risk to the lives of young people. However, it was a great deal of fun. But, not without its risks.

The Post Road Junior High School in White Plains, New York where I went to junior high school, was located at the bottom of a hill. I never took a bus to school. As a matter of fact I never rode any school bus to school in my whole childhood. I always walked or rode my bike, or was given a ride. The Pleasant Valley School in Jeannette, Pennsylvania, where I started first grade was a two room schoolhouse with six grades taught by two teachers. I can remember walking down the Spanish Villa area road to the trolley tracks, which connected Greensburg with Jeannette and walking those tracks to the school road. The first two rows of seats in the school were the first grade, the second two rows were second grade, etc. This one teacher kept all three grades going for the entire school day. Pretty incredible. In the middle between the two rooms was a big coal fired furnace supplied by the regions extensive coal deposits. We brought our lunch each day in a tin lunch box and a thermos bottle for milk. The smell of stale milk today always brings back memories of those lunch boxes.

The Post Road School was probably a mile from our house on Albemarle Road and it was an easy walk without too much automobile traffic. We would walk up past the Senior High School, through some residential neighborhoods and could be at school within a half hour.

On snowy days is when we took certain liberties about getting to and from school. The automobiles would be going very slowly at the top of the hill above the Post Road School because of the snowy roads and an intersection stop sign. We, my buddies and I, would be standing around the top of the hill waiting for the next car to come to a stop. The technique was to sneak up behind the car without the driver seeing us and grab the bumper with both hands, knees bent in a squat position and sitting back on our heels. When the car started up, we were on our way. Normally we would be on the right side of the car so that when we wanted to get off, or the driver got mad when we got discovered, it was easy to slide to the curb of the road and run like hell. The only real hazard, aside from being hit by another car behind you, was hitting a dry manhole cover and your feet would come to a dead stop. You would be sprawled hanging on the bumper trying to get your feet back underneath you.

Beer Making on Pequot Road

A college education normally includes drinking lots of beer and not learning when to quit drinking before you get drunk. Middlebury was no exception for me and there are countless occasions which would make this chapter too long. Sure there are those early drinking experiences when you and your buddies stole some vodka from your parent's liquor cabinet and mixed it with ginger ale or coke.

One of those "firsts" for me was during the 4th of July celebrations at 128 Albemarle Road in White Plains, New York where all the neighbors would get together to have a big cookout and picnic in our back yard. There was always a keg of beer which would be bought by the community and then anyone who wanted hard liquor would bring their own choices. The horseshoe pitching contests were always in progress and there were croquet matches and basketball shooting either in our backyard or next door at the Ballards. My first beer was at one of these 4th of July events when I was 12 from the keg when no one was looking.

I drank a little beer in high school, but it was not much and we could legally drink in New York State at the age of 18, which was 1950 for me. Now the legal age is 21 most everywhere, except Wisconsin and Canada. It was that fall of 1950 that I headed off to Middlebury College to begin my first year away from home. For every home football game there was always a big keg party at the Chi Psi fraternity house, where I was a "brother." The bar was downstairs and the floor was usually wet with spilled beer on the linoleum tiled floor which the next day was like walking across fly paper.

Beer drinking is input, process, and output. Just like computers. I did a lot of input, process, and output. One night in my freshman year a bunch of fraternity brothers, which probably included Bob Swezey, Alfred (Monk) John MacClurg III, Gus Boardman, Bob (Perk) Perkins, Robert (Blotto) Black, and others went down to the Crow Bar in Sudbury, Vermont with some college dates. The Crow Bar was a large barn which had been made into a very rustic bar with open beams and wide plank flooring. How they got the old manure smells out, I do not know, but it did not matter. I don't remember who my date was and she probably does not want to remember who I was even to this day. It was mid-way through the evening when we all had had a lot to drink and I was drinking beer, since I was not into drinking hard liquor. The usual output process had begun and so I went to the only "head." The line was long and my need was immediate. No problem. I walked out the front door of the barn into the pitch dark night with no moon to illuminate my way. I turned to the right to go around the corner and relieve myself of the "suds." What I had forgotten was that many barns had ramps leading up to the front doors and at the door level there would be a drop off of a few feet. This Crow Bar barn was no exception and I was in no mental state to remember that fact. I took one step into the pitch dark evening, landed on my hand and bent back my left pinky finger. I got up and took inventory. Nothing seemed broken. I could walk, see, and hear. So, I went about my business and returned to my friends inside. The pinky finger began to swell and hurt like hell. This event caused me to switch that evening to a hard liquor disaster. What all my "pseudo-doctor" fraternity brothers advised was to soak the finger in ice cold water. I switched to tall whiskey and water with lots of ice, which was their prescription. As the drink got down to the fingernail level from the rim of the glass, another drink was ordered to soak the finger. How many? How long? I don't know. My little pinky finger is still crooked sixty years later and a reminder to continue drinking beer and not hard whiskey.

A young fledgling bank trainee at the First National Bank of Boston in 1958 earned $5,500 a year and could just about afford a case of beer. Real cheap beer would cost $2 a case, like Genesee. Even that was expensive when a family of two was being provided for in the Boston community. I turned to making my own beer. I had two things going for me. One was grandmother Cora's beer recipe and a book, "The Proceeding of the Company," which was a privately published book from the 1930's prohibition era. I bought a 15 gallon ceramic crock which would be the vessel to hold the beer. The downstairs basement shop of our Wayland home at 44 Pequot Road would be the coolest place in the house to set up the "brewery ." My shop was just the other side to one of the kid's bedrooms. I tried all the recipes that looked to make sense, such as cutting up potatoes, putting in raisins, etc. for the different flavors. I bought Blue Ribbon malt syrup in a little Italian grocery store in Framingham since the local Collins Market in Wayland had never ever carried anything even close to malt syrup. The Irish moss, which gave the beer its foamy head, was also from that little Italian grocer. I invested in a bottle capper and a bag of bottle caps. The inventory of bottles came from drinking quart beers and saving those bottles, which I ran through the dish washer. That old dishwasher was an antique. It had two removable cylindrical cores, which enabled it to do double duty – one core for dishes and the other core for washing clothes all in the same machine. Clever. One for dishes. One for diapers. It was an offbeat brand which never made it big into the world of home appliances. It was also the only one I had ever seen or heard of.

My batches of brew were pretty regular. In the summer I would get a batch in about 7 days because of the warmer weather hastening the fermentation process. It also hastened the fruit fly population as well. The winter batches fermented less rapidly and the process took about 10 days. I would use my saccharometer, a device to test sugar concentration, to determine when to bottle the batch. I had cheesecloth over the crock to keep out the fruit flies and any dust pollutants. When the time came to bottle, I would set up all my washed bottles on the shop table and then take each one down to the crock level so that I could siphon off through a small hose the newly made batch of beer. In the bottom of each bottle, I would put a teaspoon of sugar to give it a little "boost ." After capping each bottle, I would put them in an old wooden milk crate that I had and store them under the shop table. Every now and then during a hot summer spell, one would blow up and a chain reaction would occur breaking all the adjacent bottles. I used to have a fair amount of broken glass imbedded into the underside of the shop table. Fortunately none of the explosions blew the kid's wall down or occurred at night to wake them.

My worst headaches came from my homebrew, but it was cheap at 5 cents a quart…and had a good "kick ."

Easter Sunrise Crow Shoot

The idea of getting up at 4 AM in the morning on any day of the year is not one of the most enjoyable ideas. Those of us who have strong religious bents feel that Easter Sunday morning is a special day of the year and that a sunrise service is well worth the effort for our souls. I was among that group a number of years ago driven by some of the same religious fervor that compelled my Hanover, NH neighbors. Only my bent that Easter Sunday morning in 1956 was to go crow shooting with Dick Fowler, who ran the Dartmouth Co-op, Hanson Carroll, a noted Vermont photographer, and Jon Strong, my brother-in-law.

This crow shoot had been hatched many nights ago and the organization of it was pretty thin. The weather was supposed to be decent on that early April morning and all four of us were whetting our more exotic hunting genes for some different kind of excitement that required skill, stamina and unusual technique.

Dick Fowler had mentioned he had sent away for a new recording which he had seen in an outdoor magazine, probably *Crows Unlimited*. That recording was "Crows Mating" and "Crows in Distress ." The recording was on one 78rpm plastic vinyl disk and when he received it he immediately played it at home on his phonograph. His bird dog who spent much of his time on the back porch, especially during mud season, went absolutely "bonkers ." At first he screeched high decibel howls when "Crows in Distress" was played. His daughters who were upstairs studying slammed their doors shut to get rid of the noise. And, his wife, Posey, was in the kitchen preparing dinner and waiting to hear the evening news on the kitchen radio. But in the living room it was like a full moon had suddenly appeared and the rutting season for crows and dogs was in full concert – screeching and howling. The recording was of superb quality and the planning for this unique Easter Sunday sunrise service was well under way in Fowler's mind. Each of us got our respective telephone calls to alert us of the recordings arrival and that the upcoming event was taking shape. We got our 12 gauge shotguns and shells ready for that Easter morning. Our plan was to meet at Fowler's home on Rope Ferry Road at 4:30 AM and he would have the recording. Hanson would bring his portable phonograph and a speaker with plenty of wire. Jon and myself would bring the coffee and some doughnuts bought the night before. Each of us arrived with high enthusiasms only to find that Hanson's phonograph needed 24 D cell batteries because the ones that were in it were totally dead. A new hunt immediately got organized. Amazingly enough we found the 24 batteries we needed at an all-night gas station in West Lebanon.

Buoyed by this success, we motored over to Wilder to the town dump in the still dark of the morning. Hanson had sighted many crows there on his frequent dump trips and so this dump would be our first since it was so well populated with unsuspecting crows. We parked the Jeep way out beyond the gate, lugged the newly loaded portable phonograph and its precious record which only Fowler, his dog and family had heard, and headed towards the dump. There was surrounding the front of the dump numerous pine trees which afforded us excellent protection. We chose a tall pine closest to the dump and put the speaker as high up in the tree as we could get it. The wire got strung back to the phonograph which was under another tree. Each of us took our positions underneath other pine trees with our shotguns ready for the first Easter sunrise event.

Should it be "Crows Mating" or should it be "Crows in Distress"? Since Fowler had heard both, it became his choice and as you might expect from his pure Easter morning mind, came the choice of "Crows Mating ." I don't know much about crows, but have you ever seen or heard of crows mating in the early pre-dawn before most every other living creature stirs?

Well, anyway, it was a hit! We had the phonograph with its super battery life turned up to high volume. The first beams of sun were touching the high cirrus clouds turning them rosy pink. Every crow within 5 miles must have heard this mating call and within a few minutes we had every horny crow, of which there were probably 50, coming in on that beacon of sound towards the dump.

We all held our positions stuck back as far as we could get into the base of our respective pine trees with our guns poised sky-ward waiting until there was a sufficient population of crows to make our journey worthwhile. Fowler led the charge. He bolted out from his pine tree cover and started the event with his pump action 12 gauge and the rest of us followed suit right afterwards. Between the four of us we probably had 6 or 7 crows which wasn't bad for this spooky clever bird. But it was an event that was over within one minute and every randy crow that had been lucky enough to have been spared our trickery was well on his way out of there.

We pick up our gear, wind up the wire, and trek back to the Jeep for the next dump up the Connecticut River. By this time it was getting light and it was indeed a beautiful morning. Our first sunrise service had been lots of fun. Now we are on our way for the second sunrise service at the Norwich dump.

For our next phonic selection we chose "Crows in Distress" and repeated the same technique which had garnered us success

in Wilder. Our hope was that none of the Wilder crow community had alerted their immediate northern brethren to our tactics.
If they had, their message was probably that if you hear some
horny music coming out of a pine tree near your local dump,
forget it because it is a lair for some off the wall hunters looking
for some excitement. What the Wilder crow community didn't
know was that there was a second side to this adventure – the
distress call.

Sure enough we snookered them again with the distress call
using the same tested tactics we had used earlier. By the time
we had ourselves all set up and ready, the morning was well under way. The morning mists had lifted. The sun was bright. The
wildlife kingdom was moving, including the rat population that
inhabits every dump.

By 10 AM we were home and enjoying another cup of coffee.
The Baptists, Lutherans, Congregationalists, Universalists and
the Catholics were on their way out of their homes to attend
church or just returning from their sunrise services on some high
promontory. I doubt any of them held a service at their local
dump. We, on the other hand, had an enriching experience, but I
shall remember mine for a lot longer than they did.

Hitting a Lawyer with '57 VW Bug

On a frosty cold December morning in 1968 I got into my 1957 VW bug to begin my commute to work from our house in Wayland, Massachusetts. That morning I was thinking about how I was going to fire a guy at work who was not "cutting the mustard ." The back roads took me up our dirt road on Hazelbrook Lane to Glezen Lane into Weston and to a stop light on Route 20. I was stopped for the traffic light heading straight into the sun just before 8 AM. There is almost no defroster on the VW to clear the windshield, so I am scrapping the frost off with my gloves to keep it clear. The traffic light changes and a big Ford Country Squire station wagon ahead of me is also taking a left, but a very wide left turn into a two lane highway so that that driver will be in the right lane of the two lanes. As that station wagon is about to make the turn, it stops suddenly and I am to the left side of the wagon taking a tighter turn to be in the left of the two lanes. What I did not see immediately was a bicyclist coming across in front of the wagon in the pedestrian crossing against a "Don't Walk" light. Too late. I try unsuccessfully to brake and I hit this man at about 10 miles an hour. Fortunately for him and me the nose of the VW is very rounded and he rolls up on the hood, but doesn't hit the windshield. His bike is down on the road having hit the bumper and is about six feet in front of the car. The bicyclist rolls off the hood. I have stopped the VW, get out and help him stand up. He is OK. Thank God. Nothing broken, bleeding or really damaged. We pick up his bike and roll it to the side of the road. I back up the VW to the side of the road and we start the process of names, addresses, and all the insurance gathering. Meanwhile the woman driver of the station wagon has gone to the Weston Police Department to report a "serious" accident with a bicyclist having been hit and thrown from his bike. The police and an ambulance arrive expecting a "near death" situation from her distraught description. The bicyclist and I describe to the police the accident scene. About 15 minutes later all the data collecting had been done. I go on to work and fire the employee. I was not having a good day.

The bicyclist is Jim Nichols, a lawyer for a big Boston law firm, Ropes & Grey, and a Dartmouth alumnus. Jim rides his bike on good days to the Weston railroad station to get into Boston. That day he was on his way to Washington, DC for some SEC filing. He went to his office first, flew to Washington and back, and was home that evening. Right after I hit Jim that morning a neighbor came by the accident scene and gave Jim a ride to the train station. At the accident scene Jim told me and the police that he was fine and not hurt at all. That evening I called him at home to inquire about his condition and he had completed his day with no problems.

Two days later on Saturday morning I answer the door bell at home and a Weston police officer hands me a summons to appear in Waltham District Court. The summons describes that I have violated Chapter something of the General Laws of the Commonwealth of Massachusetts. I have 48 hours to appeal. Stupidly, I did not call the police department or a lawyer to find out what the Chapter was referring to. To my horror on Monday morning, my lawyer, Dick Renehan, tells me I have been charged with a criminal offense – "Driving to Endanger the Lives of Others ."

WOW!! And, the appeal period has expired. Now I need a good lawyer in court with me. I kind of felt Jim Nichols or anyone in his firm would not want to represent me. However, I called him and told him about these recent events. The Registry of Motor Vehicles takes away my driver's license three days later and my court appearance is in two weeks. The wheels of Massachusetts justice are in high gear.

I meet my lawyer at the Waltham court on my appearance date and he tells me some background on the judge presiding that day and also informs me that the Weston Police Department seldom loses cases in his court. I should be prepared for a guilty finding and we would then enter an appeal to a higher court. The Weston police it turns out were the ones who entered the criminal charge based on the woman driver's horrendous description of the accident. Not the victim's description. Jim Nichols, the lawyer bicyclist, comes to the court and he testifies on my behalf to the judge that the charge was not deserving of that kind of severity. All Jim would like is the cost to repair his bicycle. Jim later rendered me a bill of $11.58 to buy a crow bar to repair the bent frame of his bike. Sure enough the judge finds me guilty. The Weston Police Chief comes over to me afterward and said he was on vacation at the time of the accident and would not have issued the charge. Great! My lawyer enters an appeal to the Cambridge Appellate Court and we get a six person jury trial two months later. I am still without a drivers license.

Eighty-seven days into this criminal process we get to the Cambridge court and Jim Nichols again takes time out of his professional practice to come to my trial. Again, he testifies that this is an erroneous charge not deserving of criminal severity. The Weston policeman does not show up and my lawyer goes ballistic when the judge wants to postpone the trial. We get our way and the trial begins. In a half hour we have completed the testimonies and the jury repairs for a decision. Not Guilty. I march over to the Registry and get my license back. I am also

$1,000 lighter in the checkbook. In addition, I am indebted to a number of neighbors, including John Beard, also a lawyer with Ropes & Grey, who gave me many rides to work and to the train. More important is I do not have a criminal record and I could continue my employment at The First National Bank of Boston as an employee capable of being bonded. Had I ended up with a criminal record, I would have lost my job at the bank and could not be hired by any other bank because of that criminal record.

And, the lesson is – Don't hit anyone on a bicycle – but if you do – hit a good honest lawyer softly.

NIC & Joint Chiefs of Staff

After my escapade with the door key in the "lost" Pentagon room, I received my security clearances from Army's G-2. I was cleared for intelligence access that I knew about up to and including "Code Word Top Secret ." The only clearance I did not have and did not need was "Crypto ." The National Indications Center (NIC) was heavily reliant on what was produced from the crypto room which was staffed by the Air Force and located adjacent to our subterranean quarters in the Pentagon. On the other side of our unit was the office supply room for the entire Pentagon.

Our Pentagon office was something like BC526, which meant we were below ground. The name of our unit was classified as "Secret" and we had a red seal on our only entrance door. Our internal security was the responsibility of Air Force located six floors above us.

I was the only enlisted person in this Central Intelligence Agency group which was headed by J. J. Hitchcock, Director, who was a career CIA employee with a Yale degree in English. We had two "bird" Colonels – one Air Force and one Army plus one Navy Captain representing the Armed Forces. Each of the services had civilian staff to complement their intelligence gathering interests who were on the CIA payroll. In addition we had a cartography and graphics group headed by the wonderfully talented Pete Kelly, who I thought knew every inch of the world and could portray any inch on our rear view projection screen in vivid graphics to the conference room audience on the other side of the screen. The total NIC complement was about 20 people, which included the receptionist, Margie Pascl, who was a young high school graduate and a wisp of a person. We found out not long after her arrival that she had a lot of mental muscle. And, there was First Lieutenant John (Randy) Randerson of the Air Force who was in charge of the Air Force crypto room. Randy went on to spend his career in the Air Force and retired as a Lieutenant General in charge of all Air Force communications.

Every Wednesday morning at 1000 hours our NIC group would put on a briefing for the Joint Chiefs of Staff. General Maxwell Taylor had just retired from the post of Chief of Staff and Admiral Radford was his successor. It was Admiral Radford's first NIC briefing when he buzzed the outer door to the NIC reception area to be admitted to the meeting. Margie had to check everyone for admittance to the briefing room and when she looked up Admiral Radford, she did not have his name in the Top Secret listing of cleared attendees. She refused to allow him entrance through the electronically buzzed locked door. Needless to say the Admiral was very upset as well as embarrassed. J. J. Hitchcock quickly became aware of the awkward situation and took personal responsibility for the admittance of the Admiral. You have to believe that some aide on the Admiral's staff got roasted for the events that morning. Margie was very surprised as was the rest of the NIC staff when she received a Letter of Commendation from the U. S. Navy signed by Admiral Radford for her role in the events that morning.

The conference room had a dark and somewhat sinister atmosphere. J. J. Hitchcock's chair position was at a large console to signal for graphics from the rear position slide and overhead acetate projectors. Pete Kelly commanded the projectors and was well rehearsed by JJ on the sequence of the morning's briefing slides. It was in this rear room where I was the "go-fer" getting whatever was needed to put up on the large screen. Most of the information was in map and statistical form created during the week from all the intelligence information sources around the world. This was in 1955 before computers (and even electronic typewriters) captured information and put it out in graphic form. Our intelligence reports would come in from Army G-2, ONI (Office of Naval Intelligence), ASA (Army Security Agency), State Department and FBI. Surprisingly, some of the New York Times correspondents in the Far East had the best intelligence gathering and reporting of all the agencies in their area of the world. Some of our photographic information was coming from huge weather balloons sent up in West Germany and floated across Russia to be picked up in the Sea of Japan by the Navy. Many balloons were shot down by Russian MIG fighter planes who used them for target practice. The path these balloons took was so erratic that you never knew where they were headed. Just as I was leaving the service in the summer of 1956 we were beginning to get photos taken by U-2 pilots at incredible 70,000 foot altitudes over Russia flying on assigned missions with specific photographic targets. The clarity of these photos were far superior to those earlier ones. It was not a surprise to see later that Gary Powers was shot down in a U-2 on one of his missions over Russia.

The NIC front door had a Top Secret "red seal" just below the electronic lock. Around the perimeter of the office was a foil electronic tape at a number of levels to detect any unauthorized entry. Any break in the tape would set off an alarm in the Air Force Security Center on the fifth floor. Unknown to most of us in the NIC was a rear "escape" door to the conference room that was virtually invisible to the eye. That door opened into a corridor and was just opposite to the supply window for ordering office supply forms. The corridors were wide enough to allow for the passage of two 3 wheeled bicycles which had big baskets behind the rider's seat for transporting files and materials to various locations in the building. They were all over the building moving frenetically to make their deliveries.

At the supply window you could observe a number of these tri-cycles queued up for their turn at requisitioning their office supplies. One afternoon one of the bikes backed up rather forcefully against the wall (actually our escape door) of the NIC conference room. The force of the bike hitting the wall broke the electronic tape hidden in the wall and set off the alarm in Air Force Security. Within seconds a swarm of machine gun and pistol armed Air Force military patrolmen descended upon NIC quarters. We knew nothing of the alarm, but were pretty scared by these gun wielding guys searching for the break in the wall and the perpetrator. We had to secure our area before we could let them in the facility which meant that everything had to be locked up in the many file cabinets in the area. Even the wastepaper had to be locked up before they were permitted entrance. The only other time while I was serving at the NIC where the file cabinets got locked up was the day before Christmas for the day long drunken Christmas party. Lorna Mae Hadlock, a CIA employee, got hornier than a three eared rabbit at that party, which is another story that might get told sometime.

The Air Force guys finally found the break, but not the perpetrator, who had long gone never realizing the commotions he had caused for the rest of the afternoon. And, we now knew that there was a second way out of these subterranean quarters.

Tuckerman's Ravine - The "Ravine"

I used to say it was a good year when I got in 50 days of skiing a year. That was when I was in my 40's and 50's. And, I had a number of good years. The highlight of all of those years was to ski the headwall in Tuckerman Ravine, which is sometimes just known as the "Ravine ." Any serious skier would know what you were talking about by just shortening it up to the 'Ravine ." It culminated the ski season in the East. Most of the ski areas in New Hampshire, Vermont and Maine would have closed down not so much as for a lack of snow, but for a lack of skiers. A perfect ski day for me would be to ski Wildcat in the morning when it opened up. Take a couple of runs and then around 10AM drive up to the Pinkham Notch AMC Trading Post and try to find a parking spot hopefully not too far from the trailhead of the Tuckerman Ravine Trail, known as the "Fire Trail," which starts just behind the Trading Post. It is 2.2 miles to the Ho Jo cabin below the lower headwall and then another mile up to the Upper Headwall. Ho Jo named for Howard Johnson Restaurants (like McDonalds is known today) was an AMC attended cabin with a large deck where you could rest and get something to eat. Many hikers into the Ravine would hike it in two stages with the mid-point being a stop at Ho Jo to take a breather and re-outfit their backpack. You get above tree line just above the Lower Headwall and leave all the scrubby stunted tree growth behind you.

The Ravine is a glacial circque which over thousands of years has been scowered out by wind, rain and snow into a bowl facing due East. To the left of the Ravine is Hillman's Highway and the Left Gully, which are both chutes with rock outcroppings on each side. On a beautiful spring day in mid-to-late April there could be a thousand skiers in the Ravine. Some would make the hike up just to bathe in the sun on the Lunch Rocks and never don skis. Occasionally someone would bring up an accordion to add music to the festivities. But, most everyone came to get the skiing experience and a thrill of a lifetime. If you were there for the Harvard – Dartmouth Slalom weekend, you would be invited to race whether or not you had any affiliation with either school. If you could spell "H-A-R-V-A-R-D" or D-A-R-T-M-O-U-T-H, you qualified to enter. Or, if you even drove through Cambridge or Hanover, you qualified as well. There would always be a keg of beer near the finish for the competitors and a snowball or two could come your way as you navigate the slalom gates. Times were taken, but they did not mean anything.

I would change out of my Wildcat ski clothes into a pair of shorts, dress down to a T-shirt, and put on a pair of rugged hiking boots for the climb up the Fire Trail to the Upper Headwall. My ski jacket would be tied around my waist. On the top of my head I wore a baseball cap and a pair of glacier sun glasses would be around my neck ready to put on when the sun got really bright. I would put oxide cream on my nose and lips to keep them from getting severely sun burned. In my backpack I would have a pair of old khaki's, another pair of socks, ski gloves, woolen ski cap, a light windbreaker, a waffle undershirt, an LL Bean Flannel shirt, two sandwiches, a can of beer, a bottle of water, two chocolate bars, a tube of Piz Buin sunscreen, a Mylar first aid blanket, a fat multi-tool Swiss Army Knife, and a whistle. Tied to the outside of my pack would be my skis with my ski boots in the bindings and I would use my two ski poles to assist my hike up the Fire Trail. I would tie or duct tape the tips of the skis together so they formed an "A ." In my better and younger days I could hike to Ho Jo in an hour. Arthur Doucette from Jackson, New Hampshire, a longtime ski instructor at Mt. Cranmore and Wildcat, could hike the Fire Trail in less time and he had a pacemaker in later years.

Every weekend the Mount Washington Volunteer Ski Patrol (MWVSP) would be present in the Ravine. "Swampy" Paris from Waltham, Massachusetts was the head of the Patrol. Swampy was a short, stocky, bow legged guy with plenty of purpose and heart. He could be called a legend in his own time. He is probably right up there with Joe Dodge, but not quite. I doubt anyone could eclipse Joe Dodge, the mayor of Porky Gulch, a founder of the Mount Washington Observatory, and the longtime Manager of the AMC Huts. But, most weekends the Patrol would have to carry someone out of the Ravine with a broken leg or worse. Sometimes they would put the victim in a litter basket with four guys carrying him or her down the Fire Trail to a waiting ambulance for transportation to the orthopedic services of Dr. Shedd at the North Conway Memorial Hospital.

Avalanches are always a danger in the Ravine. At the beginning of the Fire Trail there is an Avalanche Danger sign indicating the degree of danger in various Ravine locations. Some areas are closed and at times the whole Ravine is closed. Snow though the course of the winter gets blown off the summit and settles in the Ravine bowl which creates some very high snow depths. But this drifted snow is of varying consistency and depth as each layer settles and another is created. Some layers are more stable than others which creates the danger of avalanches occurring. Some avalanches can be triggered by some skier action above and the skiers below get caught up in the huge fast moving mass of snow roaring to the bottom of the bowl. Underneath the snow cover are numerous rivers of runoff water coming off the mountain which weaken the snow structure above to create fissures and sink holes providing added risk to the skiers. Too many of the Ravine skiers are "first timers" and don't know or sense the danger signals of an avalanche, much less know what to do if caught in one.

A typical Ravine day would be to get to Pinkham Notch AMC Trading Post around 8AM so as to get a parking space near the Fire Trail. If there is plenty of snow plowed up in the parking lot, you might want to hide a couple of bottles of water or beer in front of your vehicle to have when you return thirsty at the end of the day. Then proceed up the Fire Trail to Ho Jo to get there around 9:30AM and take a break. Maybe eat a half of a sandwich or a candy bar. But, you do not want your leg muscles to stiffen up, so move on up past the Little Headwall into the bottom of the Ravine Bowl. You then want to pick your spot to put your pack and put on your boots. The Lunch Rocks are a favorite spot, but there are usually plenty of places in the bowl to set up your "space ." After you have your boots on, you will see a single line of skiers with their skis or snowboards on their shoulders marching up towards the headwall and the lip of the Ravine. Someone before you has already made toe holes for you to follow. So, it is step by step at ever increasing steepness. As the incline gets steeper, you have to adjust your skis backwards so that you are holding them closer to the tips. At that point you figure where you want to start your descent. Others will have probably taken a step off to the right or left to create a shelf from which you can begin to put on your skis. Always put on the downhill ski first and the uphill ski second. And, do not lean into the slope too much or your skis will slip out from underneath you and you go tumbling down the mountain. If that happens, it is called a "yard sale" and the Ravine spectators will cheer and whistle at the spectacle. You may get 4 to 5 runs that day, if you stay in one area. At around 2:30PM you want to start thinking about heading down the Sherburne Trail, which on a good day will take a half hour and on a bad day an hour. A bad day is when you have to stop skiing part way down the trail and hike the rest.

Around 2PM in late April or early May the shadows start to creep into the Ravine. With these shadows taking over the bowl-like Ravine, the softened "corn" snow begins to harden and become icy. It is around that time of day to exit the Ravine and ski out. If it has been a good snow year, you can ski all the way out on the Sherburne Trail, which is a narrow, twisty trail that parallels the Fire Trail, down to the AMC Trading Post. As the Ravine season progresses, the Sherburne Trail gets shorter and shorter. So, at some point, you will have to take off your skis and hike out the rest of the way. The skis you take in to the Ravine should be your "rock" skis. Rock skis are not your high performance skis you bought at the beginning of the season with sharp edges and a smooth P-Tex base. Rock skis are an older pair of skis that you don't care if you gouge the base on a sharp rock outcrop or ski over gritty gravel. A seasoned Ravine skier always has at least one pair of "rock" skis.

The start of the Tuckerman season varies considerably from year to year. You can judge when to make your trip by when the Inferno Race is being held in the Mount Washington Valley. The Friends of Tuckerman Ravine for the last twenty years or more have held the Inferno Race, which is patterned from the 1939 Inferno when Toni Matt skied from the summit of Mt. Washington, schussed the headwall and finished at Pinkham Notch. The modern day Inferno is a five event race. It begins in Glen, New Hampshire and ends in the Ravine. You run 10K, kayak the Saco, bike to Pinkham Notch, hike the Fire Trail to the ski race finish line, and ski a giant slalom course down the Left Gully or Hillmans Highway. You can do it individually or as a team with one person on the team being a woman. For the first couple of years I, along with Peter Genereaux, helped Team Vermont on the race. I met Peter in the late 1970's when we were both bankers; Peter with Chemical Bank in New York City and me at the Bank of Boston. Steve Genereaux, Peter's oldest son who is a doctor in Wells River, Vermont, was the team organizer and the team included his brother, Bruce, who usually did the kayak leg. Team Vermont would mostly finish second or third, but first place always eluded them. David Lamb, who races it solo, is usually the perennial winner at age 50 among the individuals. The reason the Genereaux's have enlisted my aid is that I introduced them to the Ravine when they were youngsters and they fell in love with the excitement of it all. Steve has now introduced his children so it is a generational thing.

I am not going to venture to guess how many trips I have made in to the Ravine, but I bet it could be close to 100, but probably only two-thirds of those to ski. One of the better trips was with my grandson, Todd Nordblom, on a postcard perfect day where he skied the headwall and I watched with pride written all over my face.

Skiing in the Great Gulf

Al Risch was head of the Professional Ski Patrol at Wildcat Mountain during the winter months and was a landscape contractor during the summer. Al knew practically everyone connected with the outdoors in the Mount Washington Valley and they knew him. Al was an entrepreneur at heart, had a high aptitude for adventure, and was a good judge of risk.

In the spring when the snow started to fade from the slopes at Wildcat, Al would turn his attention to Mount Washington and skiing the snowfields and gullies. At one time Al started a helicopter service to the summit of the mountain to transport lazy and wealthy skiers for a spring skiing adventure not found any other place in the East. Of course in the West, you have Canadian Mountain Holidays and others that provided Heli-skiing in the Bugaboos of the Canadian Rocky Mountain range.

Before his helicopter venture, Al would drive his Dodge Ram 4x4 truck up the Mount Washington Auto Road in May to ski the eastern snowfields, the Alpine gardens, the gullies and sometimes down over the ravine headwall to Pinkham. Al was good friends with Doug Philbrook, the owner of the Auto Road and a member of the family that also owned the Glen House property. Doug gifted Al the gate key that controlled entry to the auto road since he knew that Al would respect the road and the fragile environment of the mountain. Al's truck was outfitted for these auto road ascents with shovels and rakes to maintain the drainage ditches that were strategically positioned to provide water runoff from the melting snows in the spring. Doug certainly did not want any wash outs on this private road that provided him and his family with a continuing source of income from private passenger autos climbing the auto road in the summer. Each car that paid to drive up the auto road was given a bumper sticker "This car climbed the Mt. Washington Auto Road ." Al did not either pay or get a bumper sticker for his trips up the mountain. However, every time Al would cross one of the drainage ditches, he and all his passengers sitting in the back bed of the truck would get out with shovels and rakes to repair the tracks just left by the truck. This ditch repair went on both on the ascent and descent of the mountain.

One glorious, sunny day in May (a 50 center – more on this weather reporting scheme later) I was one of his passengers up the mountain to ski the Great Gulf gullies. Among the passengers were my wife, Betsy, Brookie Dodge, Greg and Stevie Neal and a couple other Wildcat skiers. We started up the mountain at around 9:30AM and knew that it would take some time to reach the 6 mile mark not only because of the sloppy gravel road conditions, but because we had to repair the drainage ditches on our way up. We parked at the turnout at the 6 mile mark and put on our ski gear in the bright almost blinding sun. It was certainly a day for lots of sun screen lotion and sunglasses. The wind was light so we could dress lightly. We then hiked over to the Great Gulf with Brookie leading the way.

Brookie Dodge grew up in Pinkham Notch and knew these mountains well having started skiing them as a youngster. He was on the 1952 Olympic ski team and was a top notch skier for Dartmouth College. Brookie was also one of the founders of Wildcat Mountain Ski Area.

Where the sun had been hitting the snow cover, it was "corn" snow so it was pretty easy going to the gullies. "Corn" snow is when after the previous evening freezing of the snow surface, the heat of the sun melts the upper layers to create a granular snow effect, which is perfect for spring skiing. For the gullies to be safe for skiing, the sun has had to spend some time there to create corn snow. Otherwise, it would be an icy descent and treacherous skiing. Brookie, being ahead of us, reported back that we should wait a while more before skiing down these narrow chutes with rocks on each side and occasionally in the middle of the chute. The bottom of the chute provided no outrun like you would get skiing the ravine headwall. The end of your run would be an abrupt stop as ahead of you was a rock garden with no snow.

At the end of each run, you would take off your skis and hike back up to the top of the gully and take another run. On a good day you could probably have the energy for three runs, but skiing like you never experienced before. This was heart pounding, deep breathing, exciting skiing as well as memorable. You earned great bragging rights to have skied the Great Gulf Gullies, which not many people have done. It was a greater achievement than having skied the Headwall or the Gulf of Slides to the south of the mountain.

Stonier Banking School and Teddy Bear

The Stonier Graduate School of Banking at Rutgers University in New Brunswick, New Jersey is a two week on campus program for aspiring and promising bankers taking place in June of every year. The School engages Rutgers Professors as well as instructors from various commercial banks around the country to teach course material in economics, marketing, retail banking, commercial banking, compliance, and human resources.

In 1964 I was chosen along with three other young bankers to attend this three year program. One of the other chosen bankers was Bill MacDonald, who lived in Lexington and was a commercial lender. Bill's wife, Bea, has a wonderful sense of humor which balances off the family. Bill's banking responsibility was to lead the New York City banking group which included not only Fortune 500 companies but all the banks as well. It was later in my banking career in 1973 that I would join his group of commercial lenders. At the time I was tapped for the Stonier School, I was Deputy Division Head of Deposit Operations. Frank Dowd, Jr., Vice President, was my immediate boss and his boss was Bert Hassinger, Senior Vice President. Frank and Bert had recommended me for the school.

Being a two week school many of the bankers spent the middle weekend on campus. However, a few who lived close by, went home to their families for the weekend. Bill MacDonald was one of those who stayed the weekend so would have to pack for the extra days. Bea would do the packing of his suitcase to make sure he had enough underwear, socks, shirts, pants and so on. Bill, with his fully packed suitcase, travels to Rutgers to begin his graduate school banking program. We all lived in dormitories on campus which had just been vacated by Rutgers students. There were two student bankers to a room outfitted with two single beds, two bureaus, two desks and two chairs. These rooms were very Spartan compared to the hotels which we were accustom to staying in when we travelled on business for the bank. Bill's roommate was a tall Texan who looked like he could ride bulls with ease and had a big Texan cowboy hat that fit his large frame. The Texan had arrived before Bill on that Sunday afternoon before the start of class on Monday. He had already unpacked his stuff and chosen his bed and desk. You knew that because he had his belongings on them. Territorial imperative was being practiced just like on the prairies of Texas. Bill introduced himself upon entering the room and proceeded to take his suitcase over to the bed so that he could open it and put away his stuff. With the Texan looking on, Bill opens his suitcase and up pops a stuffed Teddy Bear. The look on Bill's face would have been precious to record, but the look on the Texan's face would be even more precious. I think that night the Texan kept at least one eye on Bill as he tried to sleep.

Dolly Cop Campground - Al Catheron

Dolly Copp was an early pioneer woman, who was from Auburn, Maine and settled with her husband, Hayes, in Pinkham Notch, New Hampshire just south of Gorham at the base of Mt. Madison, one of the Presidential mountains in the White Mountain National Forest. The campground there on the Peabody River was named after her and the cellar hole of the Copp homestead is still in evidence.

In 1951 the U. S. Forest Service had contracted with the Appalachian Mountain Club to maintain the campground for them. It meant collecting the garbage, cleaning out the toilets, and collecting a campground fee to stay overnight on one of the assigned lots, of which there were over 150. Up until 1951 the Dolly Copp Campground was free to the general public. So, when the AMC took over the administration and began charging a fee, there was quite a ruckus and the Dolly Copp Campers Association was very vocal and against the change.

I was part of the AMC crew of seven that opened the campground in June of 1951 and bore along with the other crew members, the brunt of this fee ruckus. We erected a gate house and a swinging gate to guard the only entrance to the campground. It was there we registered the campers from all over the United

States and Canada and charged them a nominal fee per night to occupy one of the camp lots. We also sold bundled firewood out of the gatehouse. The campground would open at 6AM and close at 11PM during the week and midnight on weekends and holidays. We opened early in the morning since a number of campers came from the local community, camped out for the summer, and worked in the paper mills in Berlin and Cascade some ten miles away to the north along the Androscoggin River. At the height of the summer camping season in early August we could have 1,000 campers registered in the campground. It was like administering a small town with all its events, some planned and others not. In the four years I worked at Dolly Copp we never had a murder, but just about everything else. If we could not handle some ruckus, we would call in Sargent Roger Gauthier, the local N. H. State Patrolman, to settle disputes or calm down drunken campers. Occasionally we had to organize search parties to find lost campers and hikers. We had to call Paul Dougherty, the local Fish and Game Warden (also known as a "fish cop") to help on these "goofer" hunts. Goofer was an AMC term applied to the hut or campground guests.

We enforced the U. S. Forest Service rules and regulations which enabled us to wear an official USFS badge and we had official papers to prove it. However, we were paid by the Appalachian Mountain Club on the Pinkham Notch payroll. That first year I earned $15 a week which included room and board. I saved probably $10 each week and spent the remaining $5 on beer.

Joe Dodge was a legend in his own time. He was the Huts Manager for all eight of the AMC's huts which then spread from Evans Notch in Gilead, Maine to Lonesome Lake in Franconia, New Hampshire. Each hut was a day's hike from each other. Joe also was one of the four founders in 1932 of the Mount Washington Observatory on the summit of Mt. Washington, the 6,288 foot peak at the epicenter of the Presidential Range.

Joe hired me for Dolly Copp in June 1951. I had completed

my freshman year (just barely) at Middlebury College and was looking for a summer job. A close family friend, Allie Noble, who ran an auto repair shop in Norway, Maine told me the AMC was hiring guys to maintain the Dolly Copp Campground. I drove over to Pinkham Notch, the AMC White Mountain headquarters (also known as Porky Gulch of which Joe Dodge was the Mayor), and met with Joe. Ten minutes after my arrival I was hired. I reported the next day to Dolly Copp. I was the last to be hired.

The Dolly Copp Campground was constructed in the 1930's by the Civilian Conservation Corp. (CCC). There was a large log administration building at the south end of the campground and a large metal bridge that spanned the Peabody River, which was blocked to auto traffic. The only auto entrance was at the north end of the campground off the Pinkham "B" Road that intersected with Route 16.

George Hamilton was the "Campmaster" and his assistant was Al Catheron. George had been the Hutmaster at some of the AMC huts, the last being the Lakes of the Clouds on one of the south shoulders of Mt. Washington. George had graduated from Springfield College after serving in the U S Army Air Corp in the Far East during World War II. George later took over from Joe Dodge, who retired in 1959, as Manager of all the AMC huts and later had an illustrious career as head of the Department of Parks and Recreation for New Hampshire, Regional President of BankEast in Concord, and as President of the Greater Concord Chamber of Commerce. George was my first real boss and I learned a lot from his example of personal fairness, work ethic, and honesty. I thought I knew how to wash dishes, but George really taught me how to do it his way.

Each of us had to take our 8 hour tours of duty at the entry gatehouse. We checked people in, assigned them to campsites, sold them firewood, and maintained a control of who entered the campground. The only time we shaved was prior to going to the gatehouse to take our tour of duty. We each had a rotating night duty tour which included sleeping in a bunk bed in the back of the gatehouse. On weekend nights we were frequently awoken to drunken campers honking their horn after being locked out after midnight and having to park their car in an adjacent lot and walk to their campsite in the dark of night usually without a flashlight.

Al Catheron, the Assistant Campmaster, was a certified forester and had some prior experience with the AMC hut system. Joe Dodge or Ann Dodge, Joe's daughter, gave him the nickname, "Good Deal." Al would finish many sentences with "Good Deal," which became his moniker. Al had graduated from the University of Maine with a major in Forestry. Al spent only one year at Dolly Copp and then went on to work for the Society for the Preservation of New Hampshire Forests.

Al Catheron always stood tall and stiff. He was a lean fellow and was careful as to what he ate. I think he loved the military style of how we ran the campground under George. One day Al was preparing to take the night tour of duty at the gatehouse. He had his starched khaki pants and shirt on. He had finished dinner in the kitchen of the log administration center which also had an 8 person bunkroom where we all lived. A thunderstorm was brewing over Mt. Madison and it began to rain heavily. Al was standing over the kitchen sink brushing his teeth and leaning over the faucet getting a drink of water when a bolt of lightening hit the water line supplying the campground from Culhane Brook. That "zap" of lightening traveled along the water pipe to our kitchen sink. There was a loud sound. It wasn't thunder. It was Al blown off his feet as he was brushing his teeth and the sound when he landed backwards on the floor slightly dazed. We rushed over to help him up and he was fine, but his false teeth, his "choppers," resided in the sink. Little did we know that Al had false teeth and he never told us how or why he had them. If only false teeth could talk.

Tony Gauba also had some AMC experience. He grew up in West Hartford, Connecticut and knew the mountains having been a mule skinner for Joe in the prior summers. Pack mules were housed during the year over in Whitefield and used in the late spring to provision the huts and to carry in LP gas tanks (known as "goofer bombs"). The mules became obsolete when helicopters took over their job a few years later. Tony was excellent with a bull whip as he could snap a cigarette out from your lips and take a quarter between your thumb and forefinger with his dexterity. All the mountain huts were stocked with S. S. Pierce canned goods and non-perishable items with mule trains prior to the opening of each hut. After the huts opened, the hutmen would do all the packing in of all goods for consumption. With hobnail boots (Limmer boots were the best), pack boards, lots of sweat and hard work those hutmen would work like mules. Tony also introduced me to a trick which always attracted the "chicks" at camp. He would take a sip of gasoline and spit it through a lighted match held at arm's length. My first attempt at the chick trick resulted in singing my eyebrows. After Dolly Copp, Tony enlisted in the Air Force and taught rescue and survival to fighter pilots in the Northwest. He also was an excellent photographer and many of his mountain scenes graced the calendars and brochures of the Sierra Club. Right after Tony's tour of duty with the Air Force, he came back to work as my assistant at Dolly Copp in 1956. Unfortunately, Tony died of asphyxiation some years later in his camper van parked in some western mountain pass.

Reg Roofing Top Notch Camp

Reg Dinsmore, my grandfather, was a carpenter when he could find the work. When he could not, he was a writer of short stories for pulp magazines. He loved both. But more than anything else he loved the outdoors and Cora. It may have been in that order. I don't know.

A number of the camps on Lake Penneseewassee have the carpenter signature of Reg, especially on the east side of the lake where he lived. Someone once said you could tell Reg's work by the large number of nails used in the framing construction.

Reg and Cora lived on the Lake year-round for a number of years. He built a small two bedroom cedar log cabin that was chinked with oakum between the logs for insulation over which he had placed long strips of cedar to hold the oakum in place and to flatten out the walls somewhat. Their bedroom was on the second floor that required pulling down a trap door ladder to access. The living area was one room with a small 25 gallon drum retrofitted as a wood stove that put out volumes of heat. At the back of the room was a small door passage to a shed kitchen that was dug back into the dirt bank behind the cabin. There was an outhouse toilet up behind the camp plus a wood and tool shed. And there was a log cabin doghouse for Butch and Spad, their two dogs. Butch was a fox hound and Spad was their bird dog. They got water from a nearby dug well, which was lined with rocks. It had a depth of around 15 feet. With a long skinny cedar pole that had a brass clip on the end, they would attach a galvanized water pail to haul up their drinking water. This log cabin was their snug winter home.

Their summer home was adjacent to the log cabin on a knoll overlooking the lake to the west, which Reg also built probably back in the 1920's. This camp was larger with three bedrooms, a large living/dining room, a kitchen with a breakfast nook and a large porch. It is 180 feet back from the Lake so water from the lake had to be pumped up the hill to the camp, which was stored in two 55 gallon drums in the top of the "tank" house. Near the 'tank" house was a one-hole privy and an ice house. Sometime during the winter when there was still snow on the ground, Reg would get his good friend Bill Young to come down with his team of oxen. They would cut large blocks of ice from the lake and put them on a sled skidder to haul them up to the ice house and pack them in sawdust for the summer. A large 25 gallon ceramic crock provided the refrigeration, which was sunk into the ground behind the camp. Nearby was a root cellar dug into the earthen bank for the vegetables and fruits that Cora had canned for the winter. Their dump was between the log cabin and the camp. But, in those days, there was not a lot of trash to dump. Plastics were non-existent. Milk came in a bottle which got returned as did beer. In later years, the dump became a treasure field for old medicine bottles and crockery.

Reg's cousin, Victor Whitman, who also lived in Norway wanted a log cabin built for his family. Who better to build it than Reg. When Reg got to roofing the cabin was about the time when he went to the optometrist to get his eyes checked. The eye doctor talked him into getting a pair of bi-focal lenses because he was always looking up and down while writing and while carpentering. It was lunchtime on that first day he had his bi-focal glasses on and was coming down off the roof of the camp, which he had not quite finished. He stepped on to the ladder, missed the rung and fell towards the ground. I was nearby and heard the yell. What I witnessed, I could not believe. When he missed the rung, Reg did a summersault in mid-air and landed on his feet from the lip of the roof. Glasses on and all.

Alexandria Virginia - Tony & Nettie

Milton Allen, known to everyone as "'Tony" was my stepfather. In 1954 my mother, Juneta also known as "Nettie," became a widow from my father's early death on May 1st from a heart attack. Nettie and my dad, Van, had just moved back to her home in Norway, Maine from White Plains, New York in April 1954 when he had taken an early retirement from The Macmillan Company. They had planned on building a home next to her parents on Round the Pond Road. Dad died a month later. A few years after Dad's death, Nettie went to work for Woodman's Sporting Goods Store on the Main Street in Norway right below the Opera House tower clock. The front of the store resembled a log cabin with its log cabin façade and a hand carved "Woodman's" sign over the door.

Tony Allen lived in Otisfield, a nearby town to Norway. Tony owned a 600 acre farm and raised apples on 400 acres of the farm. His home was a large three story Victorian house where he lived with his mother, Helen. The farm included two camps on Thompson Lake, a trout pond, and a three stall carriage house at the entrance to the property. The orchard was fenced in to protect it from the heavy deer population around the orchard. He was born in Calais, Maine, went to public school there and owned a hotel in Calais that he later sold. Tony was also an out-doorsman who loved to fish and hunt. Deer hunting was easy for Tony. All he had to do was to leave the gate door to the orchard fence open one evening and he had all the venison he needed for a year. Fishing was more his love which brought him into Woodman's Store with frequency. I think he made so many trips to Woodman's just to talk with my mother.

In the spring of 1956 Nettie came to visit us in Alexandria, Virginia when I was in the U. S. Army working in the Pentagon for the CIA. Before her visit when I talked with her on the phone about her trip down, she said she had a friend driving her whose name was "Tony" Allen. Tony would drop her off and go on to visit one of his friends in the Washington area. In hindsight, I don't think Tony had a friend in Washington, but dearly wanted to have some personal time with Nettie.

Tony and Nettie arrive in the late afternoon and we welcome them to our small apartment on Arlington Mill Drive. After some pleasant conversation, Tony says he has to leave to get on to his friends place. We follow him out to his Pontiac sedan and he discovers that he locked himself out of the car. But, he had a spare key under the hood taped to the carburetor. Only problem was that the hood latch was inside the locked car and there was no way to get at it without somehow getting into the car. His AAA membership came to the rescue in about a half hour to unlock the car. A very embarrassed Tony left an impression on Nettie and us that I am sure he would like to forget. But, in spite of that embarrassment, Tony became a very trusted friend and they married in June 1965 at the Harriman's house terrace on the Greenwood Road in Norway. What took them so long to get married was that mom's mother, Cora, was still alive and Tony's mother, Helen, was still alive. Each was taking care of their re-spective mothers and they waited until that responsibility ceased with their mother's deaths to be able to get married.

With the passing of their respective mothers, they made their home at Nettie's, expanded the living room and built the "Weasel Den" behind the house in the woods. The Weasel Den was a summer living room with a beautiful stone fireplace and grill. Many parties were held in the Weasel Den among their many friends with whom they went fishing in the spring and summer.

Tony built the fireplace himself with granite stones from Redstone, New Hampshire just east of Center Conway on Route 302. Tony befriended the caretaker of the granite quarry by telling him that he was building a memorial to his late mother and could he have the odd quarried granite to build the memorial. The caretaker thought that gesture was admirable and gave Tony full privileges to take what he needed. Tony made many trips in his pickup truck to build the memorial fireplace.

Middleton's Wedding and Dead Head

Jack and Ann Dodge Middleton got married in August 1953 in North Conway, New Hampshire. Jack and I had worked together at Dolly Copp Campground. Jack had graduated from Lafayette College in Pennsylvania, served in the Marine Corp, and afterwards headed north to find work in the mountains of New Hampshire. Annie was Joe and Teen Dodge's only daughter. Annie grew up in Pinkham Notch, graduated from St. Mary's School (now the White Mountain School) in Littleton, New Hampshire and earned a berth on the U. S. Women's Olympic ski team, but deprived of competing due to a broken leg before the event. While Jack was at Dolly Copp he courted Annie on as many nights as he could after work. One late night while driving back down to Dolly Copp, Jack fell asleep at the wheel of his car, ran off the road into the West Branch of the Peabody River, and was seriously hurt. Fortunately, someone saw the accident and Jack ended up in the Hospital Saint Louis in Berlin. Annie nursed him back to health from that accident and they became life partners raising three children in Bedford and Freedom, New Hampshire. In 1952 Annie taught me how to ski at Mount Cranmore where she was a part time ski instructor under Hannes Schneider, the famous Austrian ski school director.

I was a member of the wedding party which was well attended by many in the AMC Hut community. Annie's father, Joe, was already a legend in the Mount Washington Valley and beyond. Joe was a founder of the Mount Washington Observatory and was instrumental in making the AMC Hut system a memorable family hiking experience in the White Mountains.

One of the mountain hut pranks was to steal "Dead Head ." Dead Head was a human skull probably stolen from some medical school or found somewhere in the mountains. Dead Head was a prize possession coveted by each of the huts. Whatever hut had Dead Head, they reigned supreme. Midnight raids would get Dead Head, for example, stolen from Madison hut to be placed at Carter Notch hut, which would then be stolen again by the Lakes hut a week later. Little did Jack and Annie and certainly Joe and Teen did not know that Dead Head would attend the wedding. He wasn't invited. Dead Head was secreted into the reception hall and placed under the table with the wedding cake above. The ceremonial wedding cake cutting was accomplished without detection. Afterwards, one of the hutmen in on the secret decided it was time to introduce Dead Head to the party. His thought was that it would be a welcome surprise, but he was wrong. Joe exploded when Dead Head appeared. "GET THAT GOD DAMN SKULL OUT OF HERE." "God Damn" was a regular part of Joe's lexicon and you knew when used you paid attention. The practical joke backfired and the perpetrators shrunk into the woodwork.

Ralph Lauren and Mr. Toulouse Lautrec

Ralph Lauren is a well-known name in clothing for men, women and children as well as putting his name on all sorts of other products. And he has stores and outlets all over the world. One store in particular is on Madison Avenue in New York City where I ventured into one late summer day years ago. I went up to the second floor where the men's section was located and rummaged around looking at good looking threads. I happened on some slacks that caught my eye which I thought would be perfect for the fall and winter months coming ahead.

Now I am a tall 6' 3" guy with a 34" leg inseam. At the time I had a waist of 36 which has now, later in life, grown to be a 38. I find a pair of very nice wool salt and pepper like slacks in size 36 which cost $120, which back in the 1980's was a hefty price for casual slacks even in Ralph Lauren's store. But it is New York City so what would you expect. I look at these pleated slacks which look pretty good under the store lighting and want to get a better feel for how they look in daylight so I go over to the window looking down on Madison Avenue and get a better look at them in sunlight. They pass both tests – inside and outside. By this time Sandy, my wife, joins me and gives the slacks a real thumbs up when she sees them. I go try them on in the changing room and go back out to the sales floor to get another wife inspection. Good. Now we need a tailor to come and fit them for cuffs and waist. The tailor is found and in front of a full length mirror he does the measurements. First he chooses to let the waist out a little bit. With his tape measure and chalk in hand, he measures my inseam and records that on his order form. The sales clerk says the pants will be ready in two weeks and they will mail them to me at my home.

I anxiously wait for their arrival and sure enough about two weeks later they arrive. In our bedroom I open up the box and bring out the pants. Right pants, right colors, BUT too short. REAL short. I put them on just to see how short they were and the cuffs were at knee level. Just right for Toulouse Lautrec, the famously short French painter of the 19th century, or maybe Rafael Nadal to play a game of stylish tennis in. I am nonetheless downhearted as I really like the slacks. I get on the phone to the New York store and say that I am bringing them back for another pair as these have a "tailor error ." A week later on another trip to the City I bring the slacks back to the store.

I get to the Ralph Lauren store and proceed to the second floor to find a clerk to exchange the slacks. In front of the clerk I explain that I want to exchange them for another pair. The clerk asks, "What is wrong with them?" I respond, "I will let you be the judge ." I open the box, bring out the slacks and hold them up in front of me at waist level with the sales clerk looking at me. The clerk's jaw drops to the floor and he quickly grabs the short slacks out of my hand and disappears behind the counter. The clerk obviously did not want any of their customers to see their error. He then made numerous phone calls to their other retail stores trying to find a replacement pair for me, but they had been such a popular item that they had sold out of them.

It was very likely that their tailors had taken the inside seam measurement and made it the outside seam measurement to tailor the cuffs on my coveted slacks. A very costly error on their part and a very disappointed Ralph Lauren customer in me. Toulouse Lautrec would have looked great in these slacks.

Middlebury Bonfire

In 1950 I was a freshman at Middlebury College and had pledged to be a Chi Psi fraternity brother. All freshmen were required to wear a freshman beanie cap which obviously identified them with the freshman class. We were required to wear them all year on campus.

Another tradition on campus was to forage the Vermont countryside for timber and wood for the home football weekends to fuel a huge bonfire. The challenge was to build a larger bonfire than the game before. On Friday night before the Saturday game the Middlebury students would all stand around this inferno pyramid of fire with embers flying into the black night sky like goosed fireflies.

It was October when one of the big football games was being played at home and we needed a very large bonfire to get the campus in the right frame of mind. The Chi Psi freshmen went out in a truck to Mendon to pillage an old dilapidated barn that was rich with dried timbers and siding. The real prize was to get some of the major wooden beams for the bonfire. I was at one end of a long beam that was pinned under some other beams. My fraternity brothers were at the other end trying to pry the beam loose with pinch bars and a crow bar. All of a sudden, the beam underneath me released. It shot upward toward my crotch and a large spike ripped through my pants lifting me off my feet. I dangled there like a kid on a seesaw in the air. Thank goodness the only damage was to my pants. My underwear and vital organs survived. It was a close call. I could see myself being able to sing alto in the church choir. But, thank goodness that was not to be.

Christmas Tree Collection

Christmas in White Plains, New York was a wonderful event. Homeowners compete with one another to decorate their home better than their neighbors. The city newspaper, the *Reporter Dispatch*, ran competitions for the best Christmas home decoration and my high school classmate, Edith Lacey, whom I dated in my junior year, had one of the best decorated houses for many years. It was all lit up from the roof and chimney to the ground. Brightly colored lights blinking intermittently, a large jolly Santa standing on the chimney illuminated by a spot light on the lawn or from a nearby tree, a wooden sleigh loaded with packages wrapped in snowflake and candy cane wrappings, and a bright red door with a Christmas wreath decorated with a large red bow and huge pinecones.

After Christmas the traditional fir balsam tree loses its purpose and is cast outside for disposal. During Christmas the tree had stood majestic in the center of the living room getting all the attention from family and friends. But that attention and luster diminishes quickly when it starts losing its needles and is no longer the protector of gifts beneath it.

A couple of my high school friends hatched an idea that we would "collect" these discarded trees from curbsides and drag them into the large vacant lot behind our house on Albemarle Road. This lot had been a dump years ago and not desirable for building a home. We would collect as many as we could and pile them up on top of one another. My guess is we would collect some 50 trees, get an old automobile tire to put under the pile, pour kerosene into the inner rim and light it up. Black billowing smoke would signal the start of the bonfire and the inferno of trees. We would stand around to watch this towering inferno until we heard the fire engine sirens in the distance. That was our signal to get the hell out of there.

Interestingly, this mischievous event was later legitimized with the White Plains Fire Department making a Christmas tree collection sweep of the neighborhoods and creating their own bonfires as a way to dispose of them after the holiday. We considered ourselves as leading edge innovators in waste management.

Middlebury - First Semester

Alfred John MacClurg III and James Hamilton were my roommates in Painter Hall for my freshman year. Alfred was never called "Alfred" during his entire time at Middlebury. We all knew him as "Monk ." Monk MacClurg. He was a stocky kid from Milwaukee who had gone to the Milwaukee Country Day School, an exclusive prep school. Jim was from upstate New York as I recall and disappeared after his freshman year. Monk was a piece of work. He was a Chi Psi fraternity brother along with me. There was no other like him even to this day. One of a kind. He was in love with his high school sweetheart, Susie Darling, and they married after college. The MacClurg's settled in Marcellus, New York where he made a living in insurance and real estate sales while also coaching youth sports teams.

The only fist fight I have had in my life was with Monk. We had just settled in to our Painter Hall dorm room and had figured out who had which bed, dresser and desk in that stark, Spartan room. The Middlebury campus is on the fringe of downtown Middlebury and a short walk away. From Painter Hall you would walk downhill past the Science Building, the high school, past Egan's Drug Store and Farrell's clothing store to get to the apex of the town. The middle of the town was split by the Otter River over which was a stone bridge connecting the two sides of town. Bernie Egan ran a successful drug store on the way into town and nearby was the main ski shop in town.

It was probably early October and the weather was already beginning to show signs of winter approaching. The apple harvest in nearby Bristol was over, the Middlebury Panther football season was winding down and Halloween was coming. Monk had been downtown and returned with a new ski parka. I asked him where he got it to which he replied "I borrowed it from the ski shop ." "What do you mean – "borrowed" it. He admitted he did not pay for it, but "borrowed" it. I said "That is stealing." He did not see it that way. He had already borrowed a couple of Timex watches from Bernie Egan's drug store. Borrowing in Monk's mind was that he would "lift" the item, keep it a while and return it for another item from the store. Monk even had a large raccoon coat which he called his "Kype Coat" with many pockets inside and out. I demanded that he return the ski parka. A strong disagreement ensued, which lead to a real fist fight. Monk's big wind up swings could have done me in had any of them connected. But, I was more agile and adept on my feet so that I avoided any real direct contact. His short punches however did do some damage. The fight was almost over before it began with a dozen swings and I was on the floor with a head lock on him. He agreed to return the jacket using the same technique that he had used to "borrow" it. Monk never "borrowed" from me or any of his classmates. I think Monk was trying to get attention and this was his way of doing it. It was his way of being funny. And, he was funny.

One of Monk's tricks was his photo op. He would say he wanted to take a picture of the group. Everyone would line up with cheese smiles. Monk would orchestrate the occasion getting people tighter together so we would all get in to the picture. If you were really paying attention, you would wonder where his camera was. As soon as we got in to the right position, Monk would lift his shirt and with his two hands, squeeze his belly button with his thumb and index finger and say "click ." He was an "inny" as far as belly buttons go.

My first semester at Middlebury was a real learning experience. Not only because of the distraction that Monk provided, but I lost my school support mentor and tutor – my mother. She got me through four years of Latin, prepped me for Algebra exams and had my backside all the time in high school. Being away from home and her support, I struggled with getting good grades. I was not looking for "A" grades. I was looking for passing grades at least.

In 1950 Middlebury was two colleges; Middlebury College for Men and Middlebury College for Women. It was a lifesaver for the men. Had the two colleges been integrated into one college, all the men would have been drafted into the Korean War since the women were far smarter and got much better grades than the men. College men who were in the lower half of their class were subject to being drafted. I had a very low Selective Service Draft number and would be quick draft bait if I was in the lower half of the class.

The academic rule was that if you got three D's in any semester, you would be dismissed regardless of your class standings. My first semester grades came in and I got 3 D's. One of those D grades was in History taught by Professor Pardon Tillinghast. I had flunked out in my first semester. There was a very dejected freshman calling home that evening after I got my grades. I was heartbroken. I decided to proactively fight the history grade and approached a Chi Psi fraternity brother, Don Sherburne, a Phi Beta Kappa senior history major, and told him of my situation. My grades in class would have given me a 72, but Professor Tillinghast had knocked me down 4 points to a 68 for my lack of participation in class. Don agreed to call the Professor and ask for a meeting to discuss my case. Don's persuasive arguments prevailed and Professor Tillinghast agreed to make a grade correction to a 70 which kept me in school. Another call home delivered a much happier message. So, with a 68, 68, 70, 75 and a 78, I survived my freshman year and went on in my junior year to be on the honors list with a major in Geology / Geography. I stayed away from History and Professor Tillinghast, who was one of the most popular professors on campus.

Skiing Thrills

Alta Ski Area in Utah is a mecca for die hard skiers. My one and only trip to Alta was with some Wildcat Mountain Ski Club and Ski Club Hochgebirge friends in the early 1970's. We flew out of Boston early in the morning and arrived in Salt Lake City at mid-day. We were a group of accomplished skiers. We first warmed up at Snowbird Ski Area taking the tram up the mountain and skiing down Great Scott underneath the tram as well as BassAckwards and other challenging slopes. After our first day at Snowbird we went to the cocktail lounge under the tram station and ordered our liquid of choice. The lounge had windows into the gear works of the tram station and a scantily clad lady with her small oil can would walk around the huge gears squirting oil on the wheel cogs. In order to get an alcoholic drink we had to join their club since only members can order alcohol. Utah is essentially a dry state because of the Mormon influence on social life in the state. Each drink was served in the small little nip bottles to prevent cheating by bartenders and owners.

After our warm up day at Snowbird, we ventured up Cottonwood Canyon to Alta where George Macomber had spent a winter there working in an earlier year. He knew the mountain and it's secrets as to dry powder snow and exciting runs.

He was a great judge of the sun and where it hits the slopes at various times during the day. We skied powder most of the day. It had not changed in twenty years and never would no doubt. We skied a long traverse that resembled a rail road track out to High Rustler. High Rustler was at the dead end of the traverse and looked down into the Canyon on the Goldminer's Daughter Lodge and the base station. Once on the traverse there was no return. It was a commitment. In March the lip of the entry to High Rustler is usually barren rock with snow some couple of yards below the rocks. The technique is to jump from a standing start down to the snow below you. From there it is narrow gully skiing avoiding rock outcrops along the way. It would be no time to take your blood pressure as it would be off the scale. Bragging rights galore.

While we were there Tom Leggat, a Boston real estate developer, who was in another party of skiers at Snowbird and well known to George Macomber, seriously broke his leg on one of the ski slopes. George, who had rented a station wagon with fold down seats to make a bed, volunteered to drive Tom to a Salt Lake hospital. My respect for George, which was very high to begin with, went up another notch that day.

New York City Automat

My dad, George, and known as "Van" worked in New York City for the Macmillan Company at 60 Fifth Avenue. He commuted by train from White Plains were we lived. One Saturday Van had to go in to work on something and he invited me to accompany him since it was not a school day. I was probably 12 years old and had not been in the city other than to be born there some 12 years earlier. We took the train in to Grand Central station and then proceeded by subway to 60 Fifth Avenue. He was finished by lunchtime and we went to a Horn & Hardart Automat. It was fascinating. It was a wall of little windows with food items behind each window and a little glass door to each. It was like going to the Post Office with its bank of little locked doors however, with windows to see inside.

One whole bank of mini-windows provided sandwiches, cakes, salads, and pies for a nickel which you dropped in the slot of the door to get your choice of food. The doors were made of glass and the boxes slightly larger and in each box is a food item. When you put your nickel in the slot in the door, it releases the door to get to the food of your choice. The only employees worked behind the doors replenishing the boxes of food that were just bought. Maybe this was the beginning of the fast food restaurant movement. Innovation at its finest.

Kokadjo Maine Camping

Reg and Cora had a great love for the outdoors – fishing and hunting in the woods of Maine provided their greatest enjoyment as a pair. Reg was in his element when it came to being outdoors and he was a great teacher. He took me under his wing and taught me almost everything I know about fishing and hunting. He was patient and caring as he taught me how to tie a fly on a leader, how to handle a rifle, how to approach a fishing hole and how to read animal tracks in the snow.

One of my fondest memories of Reg and Cora is during World War II my sister, Jean, and I joined them on a camping trip to Kokadjo for the first two weeks of August. Kokadjo is north of Greenville, Maine where my mother was born in 1907. We chose a camp site on First Roach Pond behind the Snow Fishing Camps on the pond. Our campsite was on a clear site on a small hill overlooking the pond. It was here I sighted my first moose early one morning while fishing the Roach River down to the pond with Reg. The moose was about 300 yards away knee deep in pond lily pads. We just stared at each other for about a full minute. The moose gave up first and went back to foraging for his breakfast along the shorefront. Reg and I would fish in the morning and then he would spend the afternoons writing his outdoor adventure stories for *Red Book* and *Blue Book*, two popular pulp magazines at the time. He had his Smith-Corona typewriter and lots of cheap yellow typing paper to pound out outdoor stories that captured his imagination. Some of the stories had titles like, Top Notch, Spruce Gum, Plourde Traps, Barren-Land Battle, Toby and The Fight before Christmas.

Two years ago, I went back to Kokadjo and First Roach Pond to visit the place of good memories. I did not recognize the open field where we camped as it had all grown in with deciduous tree growth. The fishing camps were run down and needed repair. The small sluice dam regulating the waters from the Roach River into the First Roach Pond was still there. The well maintained road sign outside of Greenville going north on the road to Kokadjo was still there. It reads, *"This is God's country. Don't set it on fire and make it look like Hell."*

Hell Gate Fishing Trip

The Dartmouth College Grant is a 27,000 acre grant in northern New Hampshire near the Canadian border. It is a forested primitive preserve from which Dartmouth generates additional revenues from the logging operations conducted there. It is also a great hunting and fishing preserve for the Dartmouth outdoorsman and women to enjoy life in the wild, part of which is overseen by the Dartmouth Outing Club, of which I am a lifetime member.

My son, Dirk, was around 12 when Jon Strong and I took him to the Grant on a fishing trip. As I recall we stayed at Alder Brook Cabin and then drove back to the Management Center and north up the Dead Diamond River to a spot near Hell Gate. Hell Gate is at the northern tip of the Grant and closer to the headwaters of the Dead Diamond. There is a gorge with a series of rock waterfalls and sluices which make up Hell Gate's many pools and eddies. These pools and eddies make great fishing spots for the fly fisherman. The day was a bright beautiful summer day and the black flies were at a minimum due to a wind that kept them at bay. We approached the gorge carefully so as not to cast a shadow on the fast moving waters below which could spook the fish. Jon and I were up on the higher bank and

Dirk was lower down nearer the outflow eddies of the Gorge. I hooked into a very robust chub and fought it to the edge of the gorge. I didn't know it was a chub when it came on my line, but when I got it in my net, I knew it was not a trout of any kind. Jon and I decided to have some fun with this fish. We started to yell with great joy about the catch and directed our voices towards Dirk. Our shouts of joy were heard and Dirk turned his attention to the two of us above. I started to unhook the fish and purposely let it get off the hook to flounder around on the rocks. We pretended to catch it again by our hands, but kept missing. It was obvious that it was a big fish. So we kept missing and Dirk was running up the rocks to help us. Finally, the fish was able to reach the edge of the rocks and return to the waters below. Dirk looked mortified that we had lost this big "trout," but then we let him in on the joke. I don't know whether that had an effect on his attitude toward fishing or not. Today, fly fishing is not one of Dirk's chosen sports. But, his younger son, Tanner is. A generational gap occurred there somehow.

Bombing Runs on the Lake

World War II was well under way in 1944. Gasoline was rationed and you needed special coupons to purchase it. The upper half of your car headlights had to be painted black so when you drove at night the upward part of the beam would not attract enemy planes. You bought margarine instead of butter. The margarine was white like lard and there was a small yellow capsule to break into the white margarine to make it look more like yellow butter when you kneaded it. But it was nowhere near as good as butter.

My sister, Jean (age 10), and I (age 12) traveled by train from White Plains, New York to Norway, Maine to spend the summer with our grandparents. Today you would call these kids, "Unaccompanied Minors" or "UM's ." Our parents put us on the train at Penn Station in New York City and we went to South Station in Boston where our Aunt Olive would meet us. We would spend the night in Winthrop at our aunt and uncle's house and the following morning, Olive would take us to North Station in Boston to take the train to Portland, Maine. Our great uncle Frank was a railroad conductor for the Grand Trunk Railroad and he met us in Portland to take the last leg of the trip to South Paris, Maine. We even got to ride for a few minutes in the cupola of the caboose. My parents would follow later by car to be there for the long Labor Day weekend. Van would save up his gasoline coupons for the trip and because he was an enemy airplane spotter during the war, he got extra gasoline coupons for his service.

One summer day at camp we got a real surprise. I was out fishing around Bass Island in the middle of our lake. In the distance I heard a loud noise approaching. When I looked up there were three Spitfire fighter planes flying very low over the lake from the south. It looked like they were taking practice bombing runs on the three islands in the middle of the lake. I was almost tempted to jump out of the rowboat into the water they were so low.

The planes were either from the Brunswick Air Station in Brunswick, Maine or were Royal Canadian Air Force planes from Quebec. It was hard to make out the markings on the plane, but had my Dad been with me with his training as an airplane spotter, I am sure he would have known.

Fishing and Hunting at the Head of the Lake

As a kid spending summers on a Maine lake is a precious time. My sister, Jean, and I were fortunate that we had that experience thanks to our grandparents, Reg and Cora, and our parents making it happen. Much of our time would be on the lake exploring coves and rocks and islands in our small rowboat or canoe. The head of the lake provided a wonderful education in nature. Lilly pads provided some pond lilies to bring home for decoration. Under these lilly pads lived some pickerel waiting to be caught on a bamboo pole with salt pork bait on a hook. Herons would appear among the reeds searching for their next meal.

Pickerel fishing is unique. Today fishermen use casting plugs with bright colored feathers and tri-pronged hooks as their lures. Reg taught me to use a bamboo pole about 10 feet long and tie on a Snelling hook a long sliver of salt pork that had the appearance of a minnow. The technique required casting the line to its farthest point and then "jig" the bait in short jerks just under the water surface. When you had a strike, the water exploded. It was dramatic and exciting. The largest pickerel we landed was with my Dad in the bog at the head of the lake. The trophy pickerel was the length of the center seat of our rowboat. Dad took a thin section of plywood, outlined the fish on the plywood and cut a silhouette of it which hangs on the wall in the log camp.

Turtles and frogs populated the head of the lake in great numbers. They also populated the bogs down in the cove on the eastern side of the lake. Floating islands of sunken logs and vegetation provided their home. In a canoe you could sneak up on the turtles which required patience and quiet. With a long handled net sometimes you could catch one, but more often than not, they would leave their sunny perch on a log or rock and submerge to safety. If the water was clear and calm, you had a chance to see them swimming to the bottom. If your net had a long enough handle, you had a chance to net them.

As for frogs it was a different story. Nets usually did not work as a frog was quicker and more agile both above and below the water. The best frog hunting was along the shoreline as you walked with great care to spot them before they spotted you. The crunch of gravel along a beach would alert them to danger. A shadow would do the same. Your ability to capture a frog on land was far better than trying to capture one in the water. They could only jump so far and you had the advantage to cover that distance easily. It was great sport for a day along the shore. In the evening you would let your catch return their habitat – both frogs and turtles – not Pickerel.

Pickerel is a bony fish, but tender and tasty. It is best cooked in a fry pan with lots of butter in the pan and the pickerel having been skinned and fileted. Cornmeal added to the butter in the pan would make for a tasty meal taking care to pick out all the bones from the body of the fish. That tedious task was worth the effort.

Model T Brakes

Reg's cars never seemed to work right, but he had many home remedies which he frequently employed to keep them working. The fuses on the old Model A(I think it was a Model A or maybe a Model T – whatever) would always blow out and were in constant need of replacing. This Model A had a rumble seat and Reg always carried a flashlight. I think the flashlight did double duty. First, as an emergency light to see the road when the fuses blew and second, as a "jack" light for deer.

I remember one night when Reg and Cora had taken Jean and me down to the old Band Box for a night of square dancing. The Band Box was down at the foot of the lake near where a culvert is located to get into town on Crockett Ridge Road. Today there are a bevy of houses on that nice old pine lot which looks out over the lake. It was a wonderful place to have a dance hall, especially on a warm summer night with the moon out and a mirror-like lake. Coming home that night we got up the first small hill where the Shepard's Camp road came into Crockett Ridge Road. Just beyond there the light fuse blew and we were in pitch darkness. Reg, not to be daunted, reached in behind the seat to find his flashlight. Among everything else he kept there, I was amazed he could find it while still driving by braille. He reached out the window and passed the flashlight to Jean and me so that we could take turns standing on the rumble seat and shine the light over the top of the cab to see our way for the rest of the way home that night.

Fortunately, Tubbs Hill, which I think is now called Nobles Hill, was the obstacle that it would have been today. The old road did not cut the contour of the hill at right angles as it does now, which makes it pretty steep. Instead, it cut the contour to the west at a more gentle angle and came around the hill by the old Noble farm. It was still exciting getting up the hill and groping our way home that night. The top of Nobles Hills is a good place to start coasting from to see if you can make it all the way down to the stop sign on Route 117 on your way into town.

It may have been this same Model A that later had a brake problem. One of the front brakes was grabbing too much when you stepped on the brake pedal. Reg was bound to fix it himself. He got out the tire iron and started working on the brake cylinder. He turned the turn wheels to the point where he thought they were just right. He asked Cora to take a position on the front porch at camp and watch as he came towards camp so that she could tell him which brake was still grabbing. The porch was not screened in as it is today, and the addition of a deck was not there, so she had a pretty good view. Her safety was enhanced because of the huge pine tree right at the corner of the porch. That old pine had to be taken down later because it was raising the roof over the porch. Well, Reg came around the corner and headed towards camp at a slow speed. Cora was watching intently. Reg depressed the brake pedal. Nothing happened. Neither brake worked. He came right for the porch gaining speed on the downhill slope. His only hope was to turn left and circle another big pine, get on the flatter land and turn up into the slope to stop. Another miracle occurred when he made it all happen. Nothing hurt or damaged, except pride maybe. I don't know if Cora screamed, but she was pretty relieved when the Ford settled backwards and came to a stop. I think our old friend and Reg's hunting buddy, Allie Noble, probably got involved afterwards to fix them because Allie owned a garage downtown and fixed everyone's cars.

The rumble seat should have survived Detroit and the National Safety Board. They were really fun to ride in.

5-39 and Bank of Boston

This is a number which I have carried around in my mind since 1958. Some may think it is the beginning numbers for playing Mega-Millions lottery, which I should probably play some day. Bankers may recognize it as a bank transit and routing number, which would be correct. The First National Bank of Boston's transit and routing number was 5-39. State Street Bank had 5-2, New England Merchants had 5-13 and Shawmut had 5-20. The 5 represents the city and the 39 represents the bank number in that city. In the days before MICR (magnetic ink character recognition) when I was in the Deposit Operations Division of "The First," each 5-39 ("on-us") check would get key punched on an IBM key punch machine in the Proof and Transit Department for processing and then sent to the Book-keeping Department for filing. The other bank's physical checks which were deposited with the bank would get sorted by their transit numbers and presented at the Federal Reserve Bank Clearing window. The First was the largest bank in Boston by far. You could take all the assets of the other Boston banks and they would not equal the assets of The First. In 1958 we were the dominant bank in Boston. We were also the most dominant bank in New England and had an extensive Correspondent Bank network so most other New England banks used The First for depositing with us the checks that were not drawn on them. This also made The First the most dominant bank at the Fed's Clearing House. The Clearing House was a check exchange operation where the Boston Banks could present each other's check for settlement. This meant that if a State Street check got deposited at The First, we could present it at the Clearing and get paid for it since The First had already given provisional credit to their customer for the amount of the check.

A couple of times during the day couriers from each Boston bank would walk over to the Fed's Clearing House window and present their bags of checks for clearing. At 3PM each day there would be a tallying of the checks and a net settlement would be made. Being the dominant bank, The First was always a net payer with many more checks drawn on them.

Today that clearing and settlement system still exists, but many more checks are "truncated" at the first point of deposit and an electronic image is digitally transmitted to the bank on which it is drawn for payment.

There are a few events which I recall that would be most interesting to the reader. One involved a Brinks robbery on Cape Cod, the other a bank pickup of checks for clearing at Boston's Logan Airport and some others.

It was I believe around June near Cape Cod when a Brinks armored truck was robbed. The robbers brazenly held up the truck down near the Canal and made off with millions of cash and checks which were in cloth money bags imprinted with each bank's name. The event certainly made the evening television news and an extensive manhunt was on for the robbers, who were never found. The robbers made it safely somewhere where they could figure out what they had stolen. Certainly the cash part was easy to determine and share, but what about the thousands of checks that were also in their loot. There was no way they could figure out how to convert the checks into cash without getting caught. So, they decided to get rid of the checks by dumping them in one of the rivers on the Cape that fed the Canal. About two months later after the dumping, the cloth money bags were found by some fishermen. The recovered bags were delivered to the First, which is where many of them were destined in the first place. What do you do with water logged checks that had been sitting in water and mud for two months? And, by this time MICR encoding was prevalent in the banking system. So, was the magnetic ink still recognizable after these two months of submersion? The check images, which the depositing banks had created from their microfilm records before they shipped the bags on Brinks, had already been created and presented for payment. So, the accounting and settlement for all the checks had been accomplished through the backup banking systems in place. Each check had to be handled offline because they were unreadable on the Magnetic Ink Character Reading recognition machines. They were just paper reproductions without the magnetic ink from film.

We decided to take all the water logged checks to a large bakery in the North End, who was a customer of The First, and put them one by one on the baking conveyer. Each dry check was then taken to a dry cleaner customer and again one by one each check was placed on a "mangle" which presses shirts and pants to smooth them out. After these steps were taken, we brought the checks back to the bank and ran them through the MICR recognition machines. They settled to the penny. Each check was read. No jams. So, there is baking in banking. However, it is not "cooking" the books.

The second banking story shows ingenuity.

The Boston Red Sox and their players hold almost deity status in Boston. Opening day in April at Fenway Park is sold out as is every other game at Fenway. Fans clamor for autographs at every opportunity. Only a few get them. But, one enterprising young banker decided how to get them all easily and quickly in one day.

He got the autograph of every team member, trainer, manager, front office staff, and the grounds keepers. Simple. The First had the payroll account for the Boston Red Sox. When the bank statement was to be rendered, the Bookkeeping Department sends all the checks to the MICR reader sorters room to be sorted by account and for a little extra bank charge will sort them in check number order. The young Red Sox fan and bank's machine operator working on the night shift decided to take these payroll checks during his break to cut off the endorsement stubs with the signatures, and then put back the shortened checks into the tray for delivery to the Bookkeeping Department the next morning. The Red Sox treasurer was outraged when they got their bank statement a couple of days later. They threatened to close their account and move to another bank. With the help of some others in the Bookkeeping Department, we created a plan to smoke out the perpetrator. There were a limited and identifiable number of people who were in the operations chain that could have cut off the endorsements. Everyone in the Bookkeeping Department knew the story and the problem. We posted large notices around the Department saying: *"It is a Federal offence and a criminal act to steal property from a Federally chartered bank. The FBI will be called in by Friday of this week, if the payroll check endorsement stubs of the Boston Red Sox account are not returned to Nick Sapporito, Manager of the Bookkeeping Department. They may be left at any time of day either in person or anonymously."* Sure enough, the next day an envelope with the stubs appeared on Nick Sapporito's desk. We kept the Red Sox account. And, whoever did it, kept his job.

In the early 1970's paper checks were the major means of payment. Debit cards and check truncation was almost unheard of in banking. The traffic of checks was in the millions, maybe trillions. Banks all over the country used air courier services to transport checks for clearance so as to reduce the "float" time and increase availability, which they did not always pass on to their customers. That practice was the "secret" profit they extracted from the system so the bank would get an extra one or two days to invest the funds for their own account rather than their customer's account. The Proof and Transit Department had the responsibility to meet these air couriers at Logan Airport at many scheduled times during the day and night. One night two guys took the bank's van from Columbia Park, the operations hub of the bank in Dorchester, to the airport to pick up a shipment of checks coming from around the United States. They placed multiple bags of checks into the van through the two doors at the rear of the van and proceeded back to Columbia Park. When they arrived back in the pitch dark of night at the Park, they saw the two back doors were wide open and several of the bags were missing. The morning dawn was fast approaching and the two knew they had to do something to find the missing bags. They got back in the van with the doors locked shut and returned to the airport to retrace the route they had taken a half hour before. Better to find the bags and be late than to be short a couple of precious bags and on time. They made it through the Sumner tunnel with no sight of anything resembling a bag of checks. When they got on the southbound side of the Southeast Expressway around the Mass Ave exit, there were checks all over the place. Fortunately for them, the traffic at that early dawn hour was very light and the wind was calm. Traffic was beginning to get heavy on the northbound side with early morning commuters from the South Shore. The two bankers had to act quickly to recover checks before there was more traffic. It was like an Easter egg or jelly bean hunt in low light taking place. Pretty soon they could see no other checks so proceeded to the Park. When asked what took them so long, the response was that the plane was late arriving. They delicately inquired about the settlement run at the end of the shift and were relieved to hear that the run balanced with no shortages.

The old twelve story First National Bank of Boston building at 67 Milk Street was built like a fortress. It was constructed with thick imposing granite blocks with heavy iron grille work protecting the windows and massive doors protecting entry ways. It was built in the same identical architectural style as the Federal Reserve Bank of New York in the financial district of New York City. The entrance at 67 Milk Street brought you into a choice. Did you want to go down the few stairs to the lower banking floor with the tellers and the retail bankers or did you want to go up a few stairs to the upper banking floor to see the commercial bankers? In 1968 I was on the upper bank floor and then a couple more steps up to the mezzanine level where the Correspondent Banking and Investment Departments resided. I was a Correspondent Bank officer and my main job that year was to help manage the bank events and keep Carl Trempf, Department Vice President, sober enough to accept his retirement recognition awards at these events.

When you approached the upper banking floor, you were greeted by a gentleman who would direct you to whomever you were to see. The upper banking floor resembled the inside of an old European church with high vaulted ceilings and chandeliers with a large ring of lights hanging from the ceiling. At the rear of the "naïve" (maybe the best way to describe it) was a floor to ceiling painted mural on plaster of the Northern and Southern Hemisphere painted by Nathaniel Wyeth around 1924 when the building was finished. At the head of the stairs to the upper bank floor were two smaller naives to the left and right with vaulted ceilings as well and on each side wall were large oil on canvas murals reflecting the international character of the bank also painted by Wyeth. The only characteristic that separated this building from a church was that there were no stained glass windows. The Wyeth mural of the Northern and Southern Hemisphere had a unique "artists license" applied. Wyeth started from the Northern Hemisphere and worked down to the floor. As the story goes he realized he had still quite a lot of mural space left for the Southern Hemisphere, so he painted two straits of the Terra del

Fuego. Nobody really would notice since Vice President Mort Jennings' desk obscured the lower part of the mural. Along each side of the banking floor sat the loan officers. One Vice President in front of the other with large executive mahogany desks and a side chair. There were no cubicles to hide in.

The only light came from the hanging chandeliers that had a ring of some 16 lights to illuminate your desktop. At my desk the lights created some 16 images and was very hard on the eyes. Gus Williams, a Vice President with always a great sense of humor, tried to fix the lighting problem at his desk. One noon he went up to Jordan Marsh Department store, bought a floor lamp and set it up next to his desk. He also bought about 100 feet of extension cord since there were not electrical outlets along the baseboards next to his desk. The extension cord ran all the way back to Mort Jennings' desk, through the door that went to the Loan Department and plugged in by the Loan Department Manager, Stet Whitcher's, office. When Gus got it all set up, he called Joe Grady, the Building Operations Manager, and told him he had the light problem solved on the Upper Bank Floor. Joe promptly removed it all.

Serge Semeneko, Vice Chairman, had a storied career at The First. Serge was a Ukrainian immigrant. It is told that he made his way through Harvard Business School by playing bridge for money. When he graduated, he offered to work for free and if after a year they liked his work, they could hire him on a permanent basis. Over the course of his career he befriended Conrad Hilton and the movie moguls in Hollywood. Serge became the emerging movie industry's chosen banker and a celebrity as well. Serge invented the term loan. He had panache and swagger which for a conservative banking community was rare, especially in Brahmin Boston. One controversy that emerged occurred at his retirement when Conrad Hilton paid Serge $1 million as a "thank you." Was that the Bank's money or Serge's? Serge decided that it was his as I recall. Serge was a take charge individual and had many wealthy friends in Boston. One of Serge's friends was a wealthy widow on Beacon Hill who used the Temple Place branch office. Temple Place is just around the corner from the Locke Ober Restaurant, then a male only establishment. The widow had a safe deposit box at the branch and kept a personal checking account balance of around $1 million, which made her the largest single deposit customer of the bank. Joe Grady, Building Operations Manager, had just finished refurbishing the décor of the Temple Place Branch which included the Safe Deposit box area on the basement floor. When the widow went to her safe deposit box after the refurbishment, she was very distraught over the wall colors, the wallpaper and furniture. She called Serge, who met her there for tea and they chose the colors and décor of her choice. I think Joe Grady had painted it in shades of green, or, "Joe Grady Green" as he painted almost everything green. Green may have been the chosen bank color because the bank had so many Dartmouth alumni working there from the Chairman, Lloyd Brace, Dick Hill, Ralph Fifield, down to the new recruits and I was one of them.

However, one banker from Yale, did make it up the ranks. Roger Damon retired as Chairman. He had an 85 mile an hour mind in a 55 mile an hour industry. He invented a number of consumer banking products well before the MasterCard and VISA credit cards, like First Check Credit, an unsecured credit line for individuals. He thought if businesses could have unsecured lines of credit why couldn't individuals. The credit line was accessible through a separate book of checks. He also invented BanCardChek, a personal traveler's check, which worked in conjunction with your personal checking account. There is more about BanCardChek in a later story.

In 1974 a major blackout hit Boston and the surrounding communities. It occurred late in the afternoon just as people were leaving work to head home for the evening. The Money Transfer Department would have to settle their work of the day at around 4PM. This involved taking all the debits and credits created during the day's transfer activity from around the world and "proof" it to the penny. Each transfer transaction created both a debit and a credit entry and at the end of the day they had to match. This matching was done on adding machines with yards of tape full of numbers. Each bundle of debits and each bundle of credits would then be delivered by van to the Bank's processing center in Dorchester to then be posted to customer's accounts. The task has to be done daily at the end of each day which on this particular day coincided with the northeast blackout. With no electricity to run the adding machines, it would be impossible to "settle" the work of the day. Frank O'Rourke, the Money Transfer Department Manager, was a seasoned operations veteran, who could face almost any calamity and find a solution. He was put to the test that day. Because he was a fire raid warden for his floor, he had a flashlight and knew that the elevators had emergency back-up electricity to keep them operating during an electrical outage. Frank collected all the bundles of debits and credits along with an adding machine and headed to the elevator. Upon entering the elevator he plugged in the adding machine to a baseboard outlet and began to settle the department's accounts for the day so he could meet the delivery van for the Dorchester processing center. Just another day at the office with a different ending. How Frank made it home that evening to Arlington and his wife, Rita, is a mystery as the subways and trains were all stopped in their tracks. So, Frank probably took a bus as maybe he did anyway.

I remember that evening because I would normally take a 5:30PM train from North Station to Wayland. My friend, John Harter, and I commuted together often and we both looked out into the train yard and saw no red, green or yellow switching lights on. No switching lights meant no trains coming into or out of the station. That piece of intelligence prompted the two of us and two other Wayland commuters to hail the ever decreasing supply of available cabs to make the trip home. As I recall, we paid the cabbie $40 for the trip and split it down to $10 apiece. The cab driver delivered us to the Wayland train station where we got in our cars and continued our commute home. It was then that I heard on the radio the blackout stretched from New England down the coast to the mid-Atlantic states. Massive.

Thanksgiving Tornado

It was Thanksgiving in November 1951 in Middlebury, Vermont when an unexpected tornado hit the town and surrounding towns. The force of the wind tilted the steeple of Middlebury College's Old Chapel building on campus. It collapsed barn roofs throughout Addison County trapping cows, cattle and sheep inside the barns. It knocked out electricity throughout most of central Vermont. The new field house at Middlebury had its roof torn away exposing the new basketball wood flooring and causing it to warp and curl as it dried out. It was a disaster.

The whole Middlebury campus came alive with help to aid the farmers rescue their livestock, repair damaged roofs, fix damaged property and provide shelter to those who had lost it. I volunteered to work in the college's heating plant shoveling coal into the furnaces to provide heat to the college buildings so as to relieve a plant worker to work on more critical needs on campus.

I was also a basketball player in my freshman year and looking forward to playing on the new field house gymnasium floor. But the tornado changed all that because the floor was unplayable for a year after the storm. The freshman and the varsity basketball teams played at the local Middlebury High School gym for the whole season while the field house was being repaired.

Dad's Death

On May 1, 1954 just a month before my graduation from Middlebury and getting married to Betsy Strong, my Dad died from a heart attack in Norway, Maine. He had retired early a month before from The Macmillan Company and was preparing to build a new house on property he owned on Round the Pond Road next to my grandparent's home. We had sold the house in White Plains, New York. He had had two heart attacks before the one that finally took his life. The first was on Memorial Day the year before. He had rheumatic fever as a child and that no doubt had damaged his heart. There were no statin drugs then and the benefits of a daily low dose aspirin regimen had not yet been discovered.

Early that morning I got a call from mother in my dorm that Dad had died. I called Betsy in Hanover where she was living and getting ready for the upcoming wedding that was to take place in Hanover. Betsy was a class ahead of me and working for Dartmouth College. She drove over to Middlebury to pick me up and we then drove to Norway. The easiest way to get to Norway was to go east via Route 2 which takes you through to Gorham and Bethel to be able to take Route 26 south to Norway. I was driving through West Bethel in a 25 mile an hour zone and I had failed to slow down as I approached the zone. My speed was probably 35 miles an hour and it was early in the morning. A Maine State

Policeman picked me up for speeding and I had to follow him to the Oxford County Court House in South Paris to be booked. I told him about my dad and he displayed no sympathy whatsoever. To him the law was the law. I was to learn later that this particular State Policeman was so detested and hated in the area, that a couple of pulp truck drivers took out their own form of justice when the unfortunate policeman found himself between two large pulp trucks. The front truck slowed and the rear truck gained speed and collapsed the police car and killed the driver. I don't know if this is true or not, but it makes for a good story of Maine justice in the North Country.

When I got home there were a number of friends there comforting my mother and grandparents. I told Heme Woodman about my speeding ticket. Heme was a very close family friend, was well known in town, and owned the local sporting goods store. The store was in a log cabin on Main Street next to the Opera House clock tower. The following day Heme came back to the house and told me to forget my speeding ticket as he had arranged to get it dismissed.

A couple of years later my mother went to work for Heme and managed all the "soft" goods side of the store such as Pendleton clothing, Bass boots, and Maine felt "crusher" hats. She could have probably held her own on the "hard" goods side as well with guns, fly rods, ammunition and knives. She was once nicknamed "Annie Oakley" for her skeet shooting ability and loved to fly fish. Remember she was born in Greenville, Maine at the bottom end of Moosehead Lake in northern Maine.

I get recollections of Dad when walking behind someone smoking a pipe and detecting the whiff of smoke coming from the walker ahead of me. Dad "wore" a pipe and had a collection that is still preserved at camp to the right of the stone faced fireplace.

I loved my dad.

WPHS Women's Basketball

White Plains High School had basketball courts at both ends of the building. One end was for the girls and the other for the boys. Each had separate locker rooms and the courts above. I had just finished my first semester at Middlebury College and was home on Christmas break. One of those days a friend and I were walking past the women's basketball end of the building and we heard some male voices coming from the women's basketball court. The door to the building was open so we decided to look in on them to see what was going on. They invited us to play and we accepted.

I need to tell this story because I need to get this event off my chest. As it turned out, it was an embarrassment to me and my family. I just need to tell the story which some people didn't believe. My family stuck by me all the way and were supportive, but some others were not.

We played basketball for probably an hour and then left. We left the group of players and went on to do whatever we had set out earlier to do. I don't remember what that was and it is not important. The next day I was visited by the White Plains police asking a lot of questions as to where and what I was doing the day before. I told them about playing basketball in the girl's gym and after an hour left. The police then went on to describe a scene of property destruction of the girl's locker room and other mischievous behavior like soap messages on the mirrors, etc. I had nothing to do with that. When we entered the building there was no damage anywhere to be seen. It all looked like it should be except for guys playing basketball in a girl's gym. I should have been smarter and not been enticed to join them. How they got into the building, I do not know. Evidently, after they finished playing they decided to trash the place. Since I was not able to establish a timeline for my whereabouts that day, I ended up having to pay a share of the cost for repairing the damage, which was a couple of hundred dollars. That was a lot of money in those days.

Lesson here is that if something does not seem right - avoid it, go around it, but don't engage in it. Throw up the red flag.

Christmas Lobster in Jackson

Ann Van Curan Johnson is my oldest daughter. We did not believe in giving our daughters a middle name because their maiden name would become their middle name after they got married. Annie, as she is known, loves lobster even at a young age. I remember back in 1968 the whole family and a couple of our Wayland friend's families all decided to spend the February school vacation week at Mt. Tremblant, Quebec. It was a bitter cold week with temperatures barely reaching zero Fahrenheit for the whole week. We were staying in separate small lodge cabins adjacent to the main lodge and would leave the cabin to go to our meals in the main lodge. For breakfast Annie, then 12, would order kippered herring. She was a culinary adventurist.

So at Christmas a few years later, I decided to test her culinary adventurism. We had a small "A" frame ski house on the Old Jackson Road in Jackson, New Hampshire to which we went most weekends and holidays during the winter. The family preceded me to Jackson and I followed later from work at The First National Bank of Boston. Right after work that day before Christmas I went over to the James Hook Lobster Company in the Fort Point Channel and bought a large live lobster which they packed in seaweed and ice. So, the lobster and I drove to Jackson that evening. I hid the lobster in the refrigerator upon my arrival which was after dinner. I got up early Christmas morning, went to the refrigerator, got out the lobster, placed it in her stocking hung on the fire screen in front of the fireplace and waited for her reaction. She was thrilled and had me cook it for her for breakfast. Now she and her husband are very much into "sushi" cooking and dining. And, her annual visits to the camp in Norway, Maine have to include multiple stops for lobster rolls.

The Art of Peeing off of an Apartment Roof

White Plains, New York is where I went to elementary, junior and senior school. We moved there from Jeannette, Pennsylvania in 1939 when I was seven so was probably in the second grade. My first school was the Pleasant Valley School between Greensburg and Jeannette, Pennsylvania. We lived in Spanish Villa and I could walk to school. At the end of the road, I walked the trolley tracks to the school. As a matter of fact, I never in all my school years took a bus to school. I either walked or rode my bike, but mostly walked. The Pleasant Valley School was a two room schoolhouse with a big coal burning stove in the middle keeping both sides of the school warm. In one room one teacher taught grades one through three and on the other side another teacher taught four through six. The first two rows of desks sat the first graders, the next two rows sat the second graders, etc. If you were caught sleeping or horsing around, you would get a hard rap on the knuckles from the teacher.

We moved to White Plains because my father had been promoted by the Macmillan Company to work in the Textbook Division in New York City. We first rented a house at 120 Albemarle Road next door to the Kammerers and a couple of years later bought the house at 128, which was quite similar, but had the benefit of a large back yard since it was two house lots. It was perfect for a horseshoe court, a basketball half court and a large garden. I was just an average student and active in sports, especially basketball. I ran everywhere. I took two steps at a time. I was tall, thin and weighed not enough for my height so I was not a candidate for football. I was however the manager of the football team in my senior year in charge of keeping all the equipment and uniforms in condition for practice and play.

One afternoon in the winter a group of us high school kids decided to go to a late movie downtown. Billy Ranscht, Kenny Inch, Jim Valles were in the group. We saw the movie and proceeded to walk home when one of us had an awful urge to pee. His desperation led us to take quick action, so we entered an apartment house on Mamaroneck Avenue and took the fire exit stairs to the roof. Whereupon, we all took a pee off the roof. Little did we know we had aroused one of the renters on the top floor, who called the Police. Having relieved ourselves, we then proceeded to leave the building the same way we had entered it only to be challenged by a policeman coming up the stairs.

The policeman herded us into the squad car and drove us down to the Police Station. The Desk Sargent asked us our names, what we were doing on the roof and where we lived. When Billy Ranscht finished his turn, the Desk Sargent asked him if he was related to the County Court Judge. Billy had to confess that yes indeed he was the judges' son. Whereupon the Sargent said, "Do you want to call your Dad, or do you want me to make the call?" Billy said he would make the call and the Sargent handed him the phone. Billy started to dial the number and then the Sargent put his hand on Billy's and took the phone back. "Look," he said. "I am going to keep your names here and if any one of you is brought in here again, you will be charged." Whew! We got off lucky and went straight home.

So, it pays to have influential friends and travel in the right circles. We never had to go back to the Police Station again which attests to the fact that we were pretty good kids.

BanCardChek

BanCardChek was an innovative banking service invented by Roger C. Damon, the Chairman and CEO of the Bank of Boston, and I was chosen as the Product Manager for its development and implementation in 1967. Roger Damon was, as stated earlier in another story, an 85 mile an hour thinker in a 55 mile an hour industry. I had the pleasure to work with him over two years perfecting his "baby," BanCardChek.

In 1967 the bank issued credit card had not been introduced and the travelling public relied on the safety of traveler's checks to purchase goods and services around the world. American Express and Cook's Travel had the majority of the market share. BanCardChek was designed to capture that lucrative business for themselves for their checking account customers with good credit histories. These checks had a unique design with a red ambassadorial sash over the upper left corner of the check.

We did some beta testing of the acceptance of the checks in various parts of the world. We gave a book of checks to our travelling domestic and international loan officers to see if hotels, restaurants and even cabs would accept them for payment. We found American Express had done a great job promoting the acceptability of traveler's checks and we had a 96% acceptance rate. One February morning I left for a flight to New Orleans and since we had had a blizzard hit the Boston area just before I left, I did not have the chance to get to the bank to get any cash for the trip. I only had a couple of dollars on me. I paid the New Orleans cab driver with a BanCardChek, the hotel accepted the check I presented, and all the restaurants accepted them as well.

By 1969 BanCardChek was installed in 120 franchised banks around the US and Canada. However, by the mid-1970's, plastic credit cards in the form of MasterCharge (later to be renamed MasterCard) and Visa had captured the momentum of a cash alternative and Bancardchek franchised banks began dropping their license agreements.

The trademark and service marks of BanCardChek belonged to The First National Bank of Boston. A management agreement was formed with First Financial Marketing Group of Allston, MA to sell and support the service with licensed franchised banks for which The First National Bank of Boston received a royalty.

For a brief period of time I worked for First Financial Marketing Group as their Executive Vice President selling the service in North America. But by late 1969, I could see the writing on the wall was that the credit card was going to overtake the marketing interests of the franchised banks and returned to the bank at the request of George Phalen, Vice Chairman, to be the Deputy Division Head of Deposit Operations.

The service was a traveler's check that piggybacked on a personal checking account that served as a guaranteed payment check for the vendor receiving the check in payment for goods and services. American Express and Cook's had spent millions of dollars over many years to promote the acceptability of their traveler's check and the general public almost universally accepted a traveler's check as being akin to cash. Bancardchek was called a traveler's check to ride on that ubiquitous acceptability. There were two variable dollar denominations, up to $50 and $100, which came in bound leather-like books of 10 checks per book. Accompanying the Bancardchek book of checks was a plastic identification card with your name and account number. Upon presentation of the check, you had to present the ID card to the vendor and the check could be written for any amount up to the stated denomination limit. This way the merchant did not have to make change as with the American Express check.

In the development stages I worked with Eugene Olsen of DeLuxe Check Printers in St. Paul, MN to design, develop and print the checks on American Banknote paper from Crane Paper Company. Gene Olsen later went on to become the President and CEO of DeLuxe, a post which he held for many years. At one point we had S. D. Warren Paper Company of Westbrook, ME develop a special iridescent paper with infrared chips imbedded in the paper stock so as to avoid counterfeiting the checks. My next door neighbor in Wayland, MA was John Markward, an S. D. Warren Vice President, who introduced me to his father-in-law, an EVP of S. D. Warren, to get the experimental paper produced. In the end we did not use the paper as it was too expensive to produce for the quantities we needed.

One incident occurred in Boston at Logan Airport with a delivery of Bancardcheks to the bank. An entire shipload of checks were stolen at the airport one evening after they had been unloaded from the plane. The Director of Security at the bank, who was a retired Boston Police Detective, got on the case and found out that some East Boston crime gang was responsible. He negotiated their return by convincing the robbers that the value of those checks was only the value of the paper they were printed on because they needed the plastic ID cards to associate with the check to make them negotiable. It was a close call.

If Bancardchek had been launched ten years earlier, there may not have been the credit card era as we know it today.

Chi Psi Kitchen Pranks

Chi Psi was a fraternity on the Middlebury College Campus on Main Street in Middlebury, Vermont and I was a fraternity brother there. In your freshman year there is an effort by all the campus fraternities to "rush" the new students into becoming a member of a fraternity. In my case I was "rushed" by the Chi Psi's and accepted their invitation. I also applied to work in the kitchen doing dishes and serving the meals in order to earn my board expenses. We ate before the meals were served at a small table in the kitchen. Bob Kelly from Woodstock, Vermont was the master of the Hobart dishwashing machine, George (Joe) Peck IV from Rutland, Vermont was the top dog of the kitchen crew, and Bob (Perk) Perkins, also from Rutland and I did the waiting and serving of the dining room. Elbert Kay was the paid cook and had a residence under the kitchen in a small apartment. He was a heavy smoker and drinker. A cigarette was always dangling from his lower lip as he proceeded to make dinner. Somehow, he managed to produce a dinner no matter his state of sobriety. However, sometimes you could see a hint of cigarette ash in the serving he doled out.

One night when he was really into the "sauce," the kitchen crew decided to have some fun with his state of sobriety. The footwear of choice back in the 1950's was a style known as "white bucks." This is a shoe with brushed white leather uppers and a red rubber sole. Joe Peck had just worn out a pair of white bucks and we were serving ham that evening. Joe cut the reddish sole of his white bucks off and placed it on a cutting board for Elby, as he was known, to cut up for the dinner guests. The redness of the shoe sole and the cut of ham were fairly identical, so Elby did not detect the difference. He struggled for 5 minutes trying to cut the "ham ." He never succeeded, gave up, and someone helped him downstairs to put him to bed. But, somehow, he had cooked a wonderful ham dinner which we served to the "brothers" in the dining room. They had no knowledge of our prank "ham" episode in the kitchen.

Middlebury Speech Class

Ted Bovey was an adventurous student at Middlebury College. He could fly an airplane and loved to rock climb. We were both in Speech Class and our assignment for one period was to do a demonstration that would capture the interest of the class as you performed your demonstration. Ted also had a mischievous side to humor and he made good use of it.

I don't remember what my demonstration was, but I surely remember Ted's. He brought a large coil of climbing rope into the class that day and waited for his turn to perform. Near the end of the period when the professor called on him, he proceeded to the window. Opened it. Bent down and tied one end of his rope to the radiator base. He then proceeded to climb out the window and rappel down the side of the building from the second floor. And, left class. The professor was left standing at the window gawking at him walking across campus to his dorm. What he got for a grade on that caper, I do not know. In my book it would have certainly been an "A ."

Middle Battell Hall at Middlebury College

I graduated from Middlebury College in June 1954 and got married a few days later to Betsy Strong, who was a class ahead of me (1953) at Middlebury. We got married in the Congregational Church in Hanover, New Hampshire where she grew up and had our wedding reception at her beautiful farmhouse on Reservoir Road out near Oak Hill and Storrs Pond. My college classmate and fraternity brother, Robert (Perk) Perkins was my best man. Perk grew up in Rutland, Vermont and was on his way to medical school via the U. S. Navy. After our honeymoon trip to Lake George, New York, we settled in Middlebury for the summer.

Selective Service for drafting you into the armed forces was still in effect as the Korean War was still in progress. At 18 I registered with the Selective Service in White Plains, New York which is where I was from. My draft number 30-11-32-399, was quite low, which meant that as soon as I was eligible for the draft, I could expect to be called up quickly. So, rather than wait for that event to happen, I volunteered for the draft to take the uncertainty out of the process. My volunteering established my entering the service in October 1954 which meant that I could spend the summer working full time at a temporary job until October.

Middlebury is a wonderful place in the summer, which I had not experienced before as I had been working summers for the

Appalachian Mountain Club at Dolly Copp Campground in Gorham, New Hampshire. We got a three month apartment rental near the Middlebury Inn and I started working for R. S. Noonan Construction Company that was the contractor for the new Middle Battell Hall. Middle Battell would sit between North and South Battell and would be another women's dormitory on campus.

I was a construction worker and was required to join the Hod Carrier's union. Each week the union steward would come around to collect the dues right after you got your weeks wages in your payroll envelope. It was tough work pushing "Georgia" buggies full of cement over 2"x8" planking to pour concrete footings or bending iron "re-rod" for reinforcing the cement foundations. One load of "re-rod" came on a long flat bed truck and was not bent in the correct shape. Rather than send it back and get it re-bent correctly, it was more economic and timely to get it re-bent on the job site. I drew that job and spent a whole week doing nothing but re-bending well over a ton of iron rod. I constructed a jig for straightening the rod and another jig for bending it into the correct shape. So with all the upper and lower body action, I was in great physical shape. The hard work exposed muscles on my thin body frame that I could not have imagined.

On October 3, 1954 we drove to White Plains and stayed in the Roger Smith Hotel because the next day I would report to the Selective Service Office nearby. My parents had moved to Norway, Maine in April, 1954 and sold the house there which is why we stayed in a hotel for the night. I easily passed my physical and boarded a bus for Fort Dix, New Jersey which would start another whole experience that covered one year, nine months and zero days. That is exactly the time I spent in the active U. S. Army forces because I got early and honorably discharged for seasonal employment back at Dolly Copp Campground in New Hampshire on July 8, 1956.

Jeannette, PA Grass Fire

Fire has been an obsession with me for most of my life. But that obsession has got me into deep "yogurt" on too many occasions. I love wood stoves for their warmth and character. It is like having another person in the room who exudes pleasing personality. The warm glow emanating from its fire box chamber, the flickering of the flames, the magic of watching the wood start to catch fire not to mention the emitting cozy warmth is a joy.

I could not have been more than seven years old in Jeanette, Pennsylvania living in Spanish Villa. Billy Sheridan and I were close childhood friends in the Villa. Mischief could have been our middle names. As all small young boys, we dreamt of cowboys and indians. The very popular Lone Ranger radio series motivated that dream and we were either Tonto, his trusted Indian partner known as "Kemosabe" or you were the Lone Ranger with his silver bullets in his six shooter.

One Fall afternoon after school let out Billy and I decided to play "Cowboys and Indians ." This endeavor required having a camp fire to sit around. We chose a field some distance from our homes up on a ridge which overlooked the town of Jeanette. It was a simple, innocent little fire with a rock rim perimeter to enclose it. Little did we realize that a strong wind could create a dangerous inflagration outside of the rim and spread quickly through the dry grass surfaces. We were shocked beyond belief when such a wind lit up the field around us and drove the fire right towards Jeanette. We ran like hell back home to the Villa behind us. Fortunately the Jeanette Fire Department spotted this raging forest brush and dispatched a crew to put it out.

Billy and I were highly suspect as the arsonists responsible for this since someone had seen us on the ridge that afternoon. Our story of having seen someone with a cigarette smoking near us did not fly. My gluteus maximus, my small skinny butt, got a spanking like I had never received before. I got "grounded" for a week after school, meaning I had to come straight home each afternoon and spend it in my room. No playing outdoors. No nothing. Stay in my room and coming down for supper was the only event allowed. One week is a long time for a young kid, but in hindsight, a small price to pay considering what could have happened had the fire kept its course and destroyed the town. Billy got the same sentence from his parents as well. I think there was collusion involved as we both got the same punishment.

Lincoln Fiberglass Canoe Company

In 1958 I graduated with an MBA from the Amos Tuck School of Business Administration at Dartmouth College. Two of my classmates, Bill Butler and Dick Perkins, joined with me to form a new fiberglass canoe company. All three of us had accepted jobs in Boston. Bill joined Gillette in South Boston. Dick went with Dewey & Almy Chemical Company in Cambridge. I joined The First National Bank of Boston. We three had well paying full time jobs during the day. At night after work each day we drove to Watertown Square to a second story loft to produce fiberglass canoes.

Before we left Dartmouth and Hanover, New Hampshire the three of us had built a canoe mold. It was part Grumman and part Old Town, the two dominant canoe manufacturers in the United States. We took the breadth of beam of the Grumman and the nose of the Old Town into our mold design. Our first canoe was a two mold process with an outer mold and an inner ribbed structural mold. These two molds were sandwiched together with expandable closed cell urethane foam to provide floatation and some rigidity. The thwarts were fiberglass and the seats were a combination of oak, fiberglass and gut stringing. We made two models, keel less and keel. The longitudinal strength of the keel canoe was accomplished with a wooden closet rod down the center of the canoe imbedded in the fiberglass. In the keel less canoe it was the same but above the bottom surface. Eric Tasker, an engineer with the Boston Whaler Company, helped us with the urethane foam process by teaching us how to vent the molds to get the expandable foam to permeate the entire body of the canoe.

We soon realized that our Watertown facility and our two mold canoe process was not capable to producing canoes in enough volume to make a profit. Whereupon, we went to a single mold process and provided floatation at both ends of the canoe in airtight chambers. With that manufacturing change we changed the name from the Perkins Fiberglass Canoe to the Lincoln Fiberglass Canoe. We chose the name "Lincoln" because it conveyed a name of trust and honesty. Bill Butler lived in Lincoln and the owner of the loft space also lived in Lincoln. Later the company name got shortened to just "Lincoln Canoe ."

About the second year into manufacturing the canoes in the Watertown loft, we chose to get greater production from outsourcing the manufacturing to Burleigh Craig in Monmouth Mills, Maine. In my 1957 Ford station wagon the three of us loaded the molds on a roof rack and headed north early on a Saturday morning in the dead of winter. It was quite a sight. After we dropped off the molds and had a serious conversation with Burleigh we headed to Sugarloaf Mountain Ski area for an afternoon of skiing. Our trip home took us through Norway, Maine where my mother fed us an early dinner. About half way home the headlights dimmed to half light and we struggled to see our way on the open highway to home. It was a very long day and we were exhausted – exhausticated is a better description.

Burliegh Craig didn't make it happen. We then located Lazott & Kemp in Maynard, Massachusetts who were making fiberglass radar satellite dishes for Raytheon from large molds. They took an interest in our canoe and decided to take a chance on us. It was a limited success, but enough of a success that they bought us out and we became a Division of Lazott & Kemp. Bill Butler left his Gillette job and joined Lincoln Canoe where he stayed for some 15 years.

Over the years there have been numerous owners. At one point Lincoln Canoe was bought out of bankruptcy from a bank and resuscitated in Freeport, Maine. Sandy Martin was the purchaser from the bank and only recently sold it to two enterprising young men from the outdoor apparel business. It is now being operated in Amesbury, Massachusetts.

I sold my interests in the company in 1962 in exchange for a canoe. I had broken my left leg again along the screw line of my lower tibia while skiing at Mad River Glen. Five years before I had broken the left leg at the Dartmouth Skiway and got four screws in the tibia to hold it together. I was the first person to break a leg at the Skiway on January 3, 1957. The ski patrol had never had a "live" one to take off the mountain. At first the patrolman had the toboggan backward with my head and handles uphill. My wife came to my rescue and got them to turn me around so the toboggan handles were downhill and the restraining chain could be effective in slowing the toboggan's speed when needed. If they had taken me down the mountain the wrong way, I could have easily ended up in Montreal if they lost control of the toboggan.

Today the Lincoln Canoe and Kayak Company is the second oldest canoe company in the United States according to Sandy Martin who wrote a book on the company called *Paddling Against the Tide: The Story of Lincoln Canoe, an Entrepreneurial Saga.*

Boot Spur Forest Fire

In 1953 the summer was drought dry everywhere in the North-east. The campgrounds at Dolly Copp Campground were tinder dry and the fear of a forest fire was a real concern to everyone. On the summit of Mt. Washington one day in August I spotted 26 separate forest fires. The sky was smoky gray and you could smell the smoke everywhere.

A forest fire was reported on Boot Spur which is a ridge south of Pinkham Notch near the Gulf of Slides. There is a trail that leads from the AMC Pinkham Trading Post to Boot Spur and then up onto the ridge above. The trees there at the higher elevations are stunted from the altitude. But, there were enough of them to qualify as a forest of trees. Lightening had caused a fire among them and with the dry winds of the summer fueled the fire into a raging inferno.

The alarm was sounded and forest fire fighting teams were called from the surrounding communities. Populations are very sparse in Pinkham Notch so the call went out to Gorham and Berlin to help fight this out of control forest fire. Lumberjacks, loggers, and woodsmen from these communities accustomed to cutting timber for pulp were enlisted to come up to Boot Spur to fight this fire. They arrived in their pickup trucks armed with chain saws, bar oil, gasoline and beer. These tough burly guys would carry a 5 gallon "jerry" can of gasoline, their chain saw and a case of beer on a pack board up the Boot Spur Trail to fight the fire. The Camp Dodge U. S. Army Quartermaster depot in the Notch would supply rations in tin cans for meals on the fire line.

The wind would whip the fire along the tops of the trees and in no time your fire had spread a couple hundred yards in a minute. The embers from the burning tree tops would drop on you below burning your clothing and skin. The smoke choked you into coughing continuously for minutes at a time. Even a water soaked kerchief over your mouth was ineffective. Occasionally a tree would fall dangerously close to you. The lumberjacks were busy cutting a "fire lane" to contain the fire so it would not spread. Their efforts were fruitless against the strong winds. Finally on the second day, the wind died down. With the calm winds, the fire could be contained and put out. The scar on the landscape would last for years afterwards. My job on this fire was to man an "Indian Pump" filled with water to spray on open fires. I am sure all that smoke had an effect on my asthma in later years.

My respect for fire and its quick and ferocious force was not lost on me. My fascination for fire subsided and became a respectable source of fear.

Photographic Magic

Our home at 44 Pequot Road in Wayland, Massachusetts was a ranch house set on a slope. The main living floor was at street level and there were two finished bedrooms, an unfinished playroom, a half bath and a laundry / shop room in the basement. One of my hobbies was photography which started back when I was in High School in White Plains, New York.

In White Plains my photographic pursuits were abruptly halted when my mother discovered that some black and white negatives I had developed were images of naked girls in a shower. My friend, Dick Keating, had a cousin who was at a girl's boarding school. She had taken some photos in the shower of some of her friends and knew that she could not take the film down to the local drug store or photo shop to get them developed. So, Dick asked me if I could do her a favor and develop the film and print some copies for her. My altruistic nature obliged and I accepted the film for development. In our basement we had a laundry area with a sink. I could make this area into a dark room by taking a curtain rod to hang a curtain around the sink area and change the light bulb to a red bulb so as not to expose the film. I developed the cousin's roll of film and had it hanging on a clothesline to dry. After it dried, I would then cut the negatives and print copies of the negatives for her to choose which ones she wanted enlarged and printed. I never got to that last step. Mom discovered these negatives and confiscated my photography equipment. But that was not the magic I was thinking of in this vignette.

The Pequot Road home allowed me to resurrect my photography interests. I had a Voitlander bellows camera that was small enough to carry with me hiking and skiing. It allowed me to capture many moments with my three children in many different places. My friend, Titia Bozuwa, was a serious professional photographer with very special aptitudes for place, moment and position. As she grew more serious pursuing a career in photography, I had the fortune to acquire some of her outmoded equipment. Her photo enlarger was one piece of equipment, which she graciously gave me to improve my skills and scope of enjoyment. The half bath in the basement became our film development lab and the laundry area became part of my photo studio. My oldest, Annie, was about 8 and Dirk was 5 at about the time I was the most active in photography. I would invite them into the small bathroom to witness the whole development process from the acid development baths to the setting of the film in another bath. Then we would take the dry film over to the laundry area to enlarge the negatives on photo paper. We would make very large photos with the enlarger on the top of the washing machine and focus it on the photo paper on the floor. Afterwards we would take the undeveloped paper into the bathroom "lab" to develop the image. It was eerie with the red glow from the red light casting strange images huddling over the development bath as the photo image started to appear on the photo paper. It was magic.

South End Bank Robbery

The South End Branch of The First National Bank of Boston was in a seedy area on Washington Street in Boston. It was situated under the elevated MBTA subway system on the Orange line so there was a constant noise of trains passing overhead. Helen Risk was one of the tellers at the branch. She was a seasoned teller with lots of years of experience, but I bet she had never encountered a holdup situation before. I was not there to witness the event. I was the Assistant Vice President of Branch Administration at the head office when I heard this story.

A shabbily dressed man entered the branch and took his time to fill out a deposit ticket. He waited until all the customers were out of the office and then proceeded to Helen's teller window. The man handed her a note. "This is a stick up. Hand me all your money in the cash drawer." Helen with calm coolness handed the robber back his note and said; "You'll have to get this approved by the Manager." The would be robber was so flustered, he quickly left the bank and was apprehended a short time later by the Boston Police.

Van Curan's Unwritten Rules of Management

Some 15 years ago William Swanson, then President and Chief Executive Officer of Raytheon Company, published a small spiral bound book titled *Swanson's Unwritten Rules of Management*. You could order up to 5 copies free and any number over that you would pay a modest fee. All the fee income from the publication would go to the STEM programs in local area public schools. STEM is the Science, Technology, Engineering and Mathematics education stimulus program in public schools. At the time a number of my grandsons were in college nearing graduation and headed to the business world. My order of five books went to these grandsons. Some few years later someone out on the west coast who had a copy of the publication protested to Raytheon that some of Swanson's Unwritten Rules were plagiarized from other works. The Raytheon Board of Directors penalized Swanson for his plagiarization by reducing his year-end bonus by $1 million and took that money back into their treasury. A far better use for that $1 million would have been to donate those funds to the STEM program.

So, Swanson had his unwritten rules. Surely over my fifty odd years of working in management, I have some rules of my own. Now, as a disclaimer, these Van Curan Unwritten Rules are not all my own, but gathered from others and guided me through my own career. I kept a copy of them under my desk blotter and would look at them every now and then when I felt the need to get better grounded.

There are twelve of them:

1. Be hard on performance and conduct. Be soft on people.
2. Always make your boss look good.
3. Control the process before it controls you.
4. Employ your strengths and hire your weaknesses.
5. Take risks. Be ready for high speed groping and deciding on reasoned solutions.
6. Choose your business partners very carefully.
7. Inject fun into the enterprise whenever you can and when it serves a purpose.
8. Be totally honest with yourself and others.
9. Build integrity and reputation.
10. Network at every opportunity. Don't burn bridges.
11. Send personal handwritten thank you notes.
12. Be generous with others. Volunteer whenever you can to advance social values.

Celtics and Bill Russell

Bill Russell was and still is a Hall of Fame Boston Celtic basketball legend. At 6 foot 10 inches tall with an enormous reach of his arms, he was intimidating on the court. The old Boston Garden on Causeway Street and North Station railway station were within a block of the Canal Street Branch of The First National Bank of Boston. Joe Devine was the manager there and Helen Sillers was one of his tellers. The bank had just gone through a renovation in probably 1966 where they removed the iron grill work protecting the tellers and made the teller positions more customer friendly with open counter tops and glass deal plates. The Canal Street branch was an active office in a busy retail and commercial neighborhood. The Celtics had their payroll account with the bank and used the Canal Street branch extensively.

One day after the renovations Bill Russell came in to the branch to cash a $100 check. Of course, he needed no identification as everyone knew Bill Russell. He walks up to Helen Sillers' teller station and hands her the $100 check payable to himself. At the same time he reaches over the counter and with his forefinger points into Helen's cash drawer saying: "I would like four of these $20's, a $10, a $5, and five $1's. With his reach, he could have even picked up the bills himself from her drawer without

Helen even touching a bill.

After that transaction, Helen closed her window and took a break. I was a young banker in training right behind her watching the transaction. Bill was smiling. Helen was trembling. I was delighted to having witnessed this more customer friendly event.

Later in my banking career around 1983 I had the opportunity to finance the purchase of the Boston Celtics from Harry Mangurion by Don Gaston and Paul Dupee, who were bank customers of mine.

Paul called me on my phone from JFK airport one afternoon after arriving on British Airway's Concorde and asked me to put together a $12 million credit facility for the purpose of buying the Boston Celtics. There was already a bid on the table from Steve Belkin of TransNational Travel which the bank was also financing. So, because of the two bids being financed by the bank, we erected a Chinese Wall between the two bankers and bidding parties. The Gaston - Dupee group won the bidding. They borrowed the $12 million, put in $3 million of their own and accepted deferred player compensation of $6 million. Therefore, this made the total all in purchase price of $21 million.

Eighteen months later Gaston, Dupee and Cohen (he joined the management group after the purchase) decided to take 40% of their Boston Celtics Limited Partnership public through an initial public offering agented by Smith Barney. The market capitalization on that first trading day amounted to $132 million. It was a home run to borrow a baseball term.

And, since the public stock offering was done in the holiday season right after Thanksgiving, every father, grandfather and uncle wanted to buy 1 share at $18 a share for their son/daughter, grandson/granddaughter or nephew/niece. The bank's stock transfer department was the busiest it had ever been. They issued more share certificates than General Motors in that period of time.

1938 Chevy Truck at Dolly Copp Campground

"*I think I can. I think I can,*" said the Little Engine that Could. We are in the Dolly Copp Campground in Gorham, New Hampshire and I have just joined the work crew of six young men to maintain and manage the campground for the summer in 1951. Our job is to empty the trash cans located in multiple places among the 158 camping sites, clean out the toilets (aka "crappers"), check in and out the campers on their respective camp sites, mow the fields, check the water supply for contaminants and send in the results to the State Health Department, and generally maintain order in the campground. We had only one truck, a forest green 1939 Chevrolet pickup truck, at our disposal to do the hauling. Each day two of us were assigned to do the trash pick up and haul it to the dump in Gorham some 8 miles north of the campground off Route 16. I don't recall the mileage on the truck, but it was right up there close to 100,000 miles I am sure. It was a manual shift transmission which was pretty simple. Automatic transmissions were just beginning to appear on the automotive scene like the Ford-o-Matic. But our pickup would and could do the job very nicely.

The summer of 1953 was hot and dry. The woods were tinder dry around us and the trails were dusty leading out from the campground up to Mt. Madison on the Great Gulf Trail or to the Imp, a rock outcrop profile, across Route 16 from the campground on the Imp Trail. One August day I was on the summit of Mt. Washington, the 6,288 foot peak at the center of the White Mountain National Forest, and I counted 26 separate forest fires burning in the distance. I was outfitting a fire fighting crew that would fight a fire on the Webster Cliffs. It was easier to supply them with Indian pumps, polaskis and chain saws from the summit rather than for them to hike up from Crawford Notch to the west on Route 302.

Many of the firefighters were from the Gorham, Cascade, and Berlin area and were used to working in the woods for the paper mills that lined the Androscoggin River. They are a tough bunch of guys who work hard and play hard. They would each bring their chain saw, a 5 gallon Jerry can of gasoline and a case of beer on their backpack. The Mt. Washington Stage wagons would transport them up the Auto Road from the Glen House on Route 16 so they could hike down from the summit.

Also, at Camp Dodge, just north of the Glen House was a U. S. Army Quartermaster camp which had about 50 men assigned there to test winter equipment in the summer. In 1951, my first summer working at Dolly Copp, we would see these hot sweaty soldiers in formation cross the Peabody River on the old rusted iron bridge that was closed to auto traffic, but allowed foot traffic. The men had on winter parkas with fur hoods, high top mountain boots, a rifle, a canteen and an ammunition belt which they were testing for the Quartermaster Corp. None of them had a smile on their face. These soldiers were also pressed into fighting fires in Pinkham Notch. So they got some combat duty. The fires were their enemy that hot summer.

From many locations around the White Mountain National Forest there were fire fighting caches positioned to supply fire fighting tools to those who would be fighting the fires. But, with good reason, there were no caches at the rocky, barren summit.

To fight the fire on the Webster Cliffs two of our Dolly Copp crew were ordered to haul as many caches as we could in the Chevy pickup truck. I was one of the two chosen to do this job and we could get two caches into the bed of the truck and drive them up the Mt. Washington Auto Road to the summit. We made three trips one day to the summit. The auto road is 8 miles up mostly gravel roadbed and only a small portion of the road from the gate house in Glen is paved. We passed Lincolns and Cadillac's on the way up whose engines had over heated or on the way down whose brakes were smoking from all the braking required on the treacherous turns. Our Chevy kept right on going. The truck never overheated or had the brakes fade from over braking on the twisty challenging road down the mountain. We were very proud of our truck and there was probably a big smile on the grille. There was certainly a smile on our faces.

Dartmouth College Grant's Alder Brook Cabin

Alder Brook is a remote and primitive cabin in the Dartmouth College Grant, which is a 27,000 acre area north of Errol, New Hampshire deeded to the College by the State of New Hampshire in the 1700's. It's northern border is on the Canadian line. There are two main rivers, the Dead Diamond and the Swift Diamond that run through the property and they both feed the Umbagog and Magalloway watersheds. The College Grant is managed by Dartmouth College and the Dartmouth Outing Club, of which I am a lifetime member. It is a haven for outdoorsmen and women who love wilderness and primitive environments, although there is a small air strip near the entrance to the Grant. The Miller-Quinn air strip is named for Dr. Ralph Miller and Dr. Robert Quinn, who perished in February 1959 during an emergency medical flight to Whitefield, New Hampshire from Hanover. They got caught in a severe snow squall on their return, their carburetor iced up, and they went down in the Pemigewasset Wilderness. Both perished without being found after weeks of hunting northern New Hampshire by the Air National Guard, the Dartmouth community of administration, faculty and students and the local Hanover community. Drs. Miller and Quinn survived the crash. They made snowshoes out of sapling branches and surgical tape. Temperatures at night reached sub-zero levels. It was a new plane, a Piper Comanche, they were flying that day. Dr. Miller's other plane had carried him to the northern reaches of the artic and was well equipped with survival gear. He had not yet transferred that gear over to this new plane which was painted white and hardly visible from the air because of the snow cover in the woods where they went down. If they had gotten to an old logging road and a Forest Service cabin a short distance away and followed that road out, they possibly could have been found and survived.

For 17 years I hunted in the Dartmouth Grant. The core group included Jon Strong, Dick Fowler, Squeak Piane, Inch Pierce, and Dick Brace. I shall always remember the first year at Alder Brook. Dick Brace arrived in the afternoon from his home in Dover, Massachusetts, but the rest of us had got an early morning start from Hanover. We got to Alder Brook at mid-morning. Jon and I had bought all the groceries and provisions for the 4 day stay. Dick Fowler brought the dirty magazines. We split all the expenses among us. When Brace arrived there was little to do in preparing the cabin as the water had been hauled up from the stream and the cord wood had been split and brought into the cabin. So, Brace went deer hunting. Shortly after he entered the woods, he spotted and shot a deer. He dressed out the deer and hung it at the cabin. There was still plenty of daylight left in the day, so out he goes again, spots a bear, shoots the bear, dresses it out and hangs it next to his deer. So with a deer and a bear bagged all that is left is to go bird hunting for the remainder of the day. And, he comes in with a partridge. It was the "hat trick" in hunting – a three bagger. Hence, Brace's reputation as a hunter was forever etched in all our memories.

The Alder Brook Cabin lies to the west of the main entrance upriver on the Swift Diamond. It was in 1957 the most spartan and remote of the Grant cabins. You approach the Grant from Wentworth Location, which is north of the Thirteen Mile Woods on the Androscoggin River. The entry road is controlled by a gate with a gatekeeper and a special pass issued by the Dartmouth Outing Club is needed to gain entry. Once the credentialing is complete, the gatekeeper raises the gate allowing you to proceed to the bridge over the Dead Diamond River. You pass the Miller – Quinn air strip on the right and at the first major fork in the road is the Management Center which Sam Brungot runs. After you leave him, you are one fifth of whiskey lighter in return for all his intelligence on where the deer are in the Grant. You take the left road taking you west along the Swift Diamond River. About three miles on this road, which is an old logging road, is another fork in the road which takes you north towards the Alder Brook cabin. Some years you can drive right up to the cabin, but more often than not, you park at the bottom of the hill because of the snow depth in the woods. The cabin has room for 6 people in bunk beds stacked three high. A wood stove keeps the place warm. An outhouse out back handled all the toilet needs. And, you hope the last group there left plenty of firewood for the next group.

We had two major hunting areas. The easiest was to follow the Alder Brook upstream and fan out so that each of us was about 100 yards apart to do a sweep of the terrain. We would meet up for lunch and plan the afternoon hunt which generally was west and down towards the Swift Diamond River and home along the logging road that paralleled the river. The second was to canoe across the Swift Diamond River and hunt the area south of the river, which very few people hunt. When we were hunting out of Alder Brook there was probably nobody within 5 miles of us. We trusted each other. We had learned to hunt from relatives who taught us all the safety precautions for safe hunting. One year we had an invited guest who when emptying his rifle accidently fired a round off through the roof of the cabin porch. He was never invited back. My success was sporadic. Out of the 17 years, I probably came home with 8 deer. I always came home with a small Christmas tree however. I would send the deer hide off to a taxidermist in Glover, Vermont to get deer leather skin which I would use as elbow patches or shoulder patches on hunting clothes. Some years I would send the uncured hide off to Saranac Glove Company in Littleton, New Hampshire and get a pair of deer hide gloves in return. The Vermont taxidermist always insisted on sending the salted hide to him on a Monday so it would not sit in the local Post Office over the weekend and stink up the place.

Grand Central Station's Newsreel Theatre

World War II had just ended in 1945. I was 13 and living in White Plains, New York because Dad had a job in New York City with the Macmillan Company on Fifth Avenue. He would commute by train into Grand Central Station on 42nd Street and take the subway downtown.

One Saturday I accompanied him into the city because he had a few things to do at the office that morning. Afterwards, we would go to lunch somewhere interesting, like Fraunces Tavern or an Horn & Hardart Automat (today's McDonalds). We would then get back to Grand Central and catch a train home. Right after the war, I remember we had some time to kill and went up to the mezzanine level to the Pathe Newsreel Theater to catch 15 minutes of continuous news on the screen. This particular time Pathe was showing some captured German film of the prison camps where the Jews were exterminated in the gas chambers and then buried in mass graves like stacked cordwood. Their naked emaciated bodies were unrecognizable as to sex of the victim since their taunt skin was hugging what was left of their skeletal frame. These were men, women and children in great numbers being exterminated and the Germans had filmed them in the gas chambers and during their burial. I was sick to my stomach. I had never witnessed such an atrocity. It is an image for life. You can not erase it. It is indelibly etched in memory. Today in these times such films would not be allowed to be shown and this one certainly would not be a PG-13.

Reg Remembrances

Reg Dinsmore was an agile fellow. His BMI, which was not even measured in his day, would be well under 25, meaning he was not obese. Far from it. I don't think there was an ounce of fat on Reg. He was an active person who could do anything he set out to do. He knew the law of physics not because he was taught them, but because he had an inherent feel for how things worked.

Our camp in Maine is on lakefront property. On the shoreline Reg built a wharf which was anchored by a rock structure. Many of the rocks that make up that wharf could weigh a couple of hundred pounds. Through the buoyancy of the water and the leverage afforded by a crowbar, Reg could create a rock wharf just like the pharaohs did in Egypt with their pyramids. He had an uncanny sense of weight and how to leverage weight with his arms and body. Watching him work was a marvel in human muscle dexterity.

One of my remembrances of Reg would be at the breakfast table. Wheaties was his normal cereal of choice. This was long before you had famous athletes on the front of the box. Reg would open up the box of Wheaties and pour a healthy portion of cereal into his bowl. Before he would pour milk onto the cereal, he would take his fist and crush the brittle Wheaties flakes into a mini-Wheaties mixture. Why he did this I do not know. But it was a ritual he went through every time he ate Wheaties for breakfast.

Beer was a favorite beverage for Reg. During Prohibition, Cora had a recipe to make homemade beer. It is a recipe I replicated when I first starting making my own beer in the 1960's. Reg would uncap the bottle and pour the beer into a glass. The glass would be tilted on a 45 degree angle to reduce the creation of foam as he poured it from the bottle to the glass. After he finished pouring the beer, he would take a salt shaker and add a couple dashes of salt. Of course the foam created from the salt would erupt and spew over the side of the glass.

Reg had a couple of goats and believed his health would be improved if he drank goat's milk. Every evening someone would have to milk the goats. That duty could fall to either my sister or to me, if Reg was not around to do the "milking."

Regulation cake was his favorite cake. Cora would make it with an endless supply for Reg's lunches. It is basically a spice cake. Moist and rich. It was not the spice cake that attracted Reg so much as the chocolate frosting on top. It had to be one-third cake and two-thirds rich chocolate frosting to meet his demands. The chocolate was so rich it made your teeth ache. But, it was good.

Reg had a green accountant's eye shade. During the summer when he was not on a job carpentering, he was down at the log camp writing. He sat at a desk near the front door (it was so small that everything was near the front door) with a single drop light with a green glass shade. Reg with his green cellouid eyeshade perched on his bald head underneath the green lampshade made him look just like a poker dealer at the tables in Las Vegas.

When you got into a canoe with Reg, you did it his way. Reg had a pair of canoe shoes from L. L. Bean that were leather uppers with a zipper and soft smooth non-tread soles. L. L. Bean had manufactured these canoe shoes specifically for outdoorsmen who had cedar ribbed canvas covered canoes. The shoes were designed so that they would not puncture or damage the cedar planking of the canoe. However great they were in a canoe, they were treacherous climbing up a bank under a pine tree. The pine needles were like ice which made your ascent up the hill dangerous, especially if you had a load to carry.

Dogs in my Life

My favorite dog is Porter who was my beloved friend for almost 10 years. She was a chocolate lab with a white blaze on her chest. We got Porter in Marblehead from Peter and Debbie Fadden. Peter is a lobster fisherman and Debbie in addition to raising two children from time to time bred dogs. My wife, Sandy was having lunch with Marilyn Doolittle, also known as Lobster Lady, and two other friends, Pam Greene and Nagisa Nara, when Marilyn mentioned that Debbie Fadden's lab, Maddie, had just delivered her pups which were for sale. We recently had to put down Penny, a golden retriever, who was a wonderful dog. I gave Penny to Sandy for Valentine's Day shortly after we got married in 1982. Sandy was smitten with Porter and succumbed to the lure of having another dog. At six weeks old we picked up Porter from the Fadden's to bring home and also to introduce her to the camp as well as the lake. For one whole year Porter would not go into the water. What chocolate lab doesn't like water? It was one year and four days before she was swimming gleefully in the lake. Porter got her name from the Black Bear Porter beer at the Sunday River Brewery. We had her with us when we stopped at the Brewery for lunch out on the side deck. Sandy ordered a Black Bear Porter and the color of the beer matched Porter's coat. Perfect match and dog name.

This is the poem I wrote after we had to put her down from a fast moving cancerous tumor in June 2010.

My dog, Porter, is named after Porter beer
An ultrasound yesterday diagnosed her with my greatest fear
The dreaded C – terminal cancer
And now I want to keep her forever near

Porter, my chocolate lab
Proud and stubborn when she wants to be
Sweet and dear more often than not
And now I want to keep her forever near

Porter is my favorite dog in the world
She rides shotgun in my truck
Looks through the windshield world with great delight
And now I want to keep her forever near

Porter got her name at the Sunday River Pub as a pup
All it took was one look at the Black Bear Porter beer
She grew up to be big bodied, malty & hoppy too
And now I want to keep her forever near

Beer and dogs. Dogs and beer. Forever near
Both are man's best friend. It was meant to be
Add the truck and you have the best damn team
And now I want to keep her forever near

I am going to lose part of that team to the heavens in the sky
With tears running down my cheeks. Beer on my lips. Porter in
my mind
I know I always will
Want to keep her forever near

Goodbye, Porter dear, Goodbye till I see you again in the sky
But you have to wait until I die Goodbye, dear friend, goodbye.

LXXX - *Latin for 80*

I took four years of Latin in High School. My teacher, Ms. Savage, was anything but savage. She was a kind grey haired dedicated teacher with a lot of empathy and patience. Patience was the quality which I certainly tested her on in class as I did not take naturally to the language. If it was not for my mother helping with my homework every night, I would not have passed the course each year.

So, when I got to Middlebury College, I had to choose a required language course. Middlebury College prided itself on its language courses. Why not Spanish? It is a romance based language from Latin derivatives and I should be able to do well in the course with four years of Latin behind me. Well, that did not turn out to be the case. Sam Guarnaccia was my Spanish teacher. Sam was the assistant football coach with a stocky barrel chest who would walk across the campus on a sub-zero morning with only a sport jacket on for warmth. He was tough. But, Sam also had a soft side. I was struggling in his Spanish course and we both knew it. Near the end of the semester, Sam took me aside and said, "Chris, I will give you a passing grade in this course if you promise not to take it next semester." I said, "Professor, you got a deal."

I turned 80 on July 19, 2012 and my family put together a celebration that I shall never forget. The night before my birthday, my 3 children invited me and Sandy to dinner at 76 Pleasant Restaurant in Norway, Maine. Near the end of the dinner before dessert they said I had to be down on the dock at 7AM sharp. They must have repeated the request at least 3 times to make sure I understood their request.

So, the next morning I am on the dock at 7AM witnessing a clear bright blue sky and the lake almost mirror-like with no wind. I am standing around wondering why in hell are they getting me down on the dock so early in the morning. None of them are fishermen and normal activity – like drinking your first cup of coffee - doesn't take place usually before 8 or so in the morning. Well after about 15 minutes of standing around, they bring out a brand new blue kayak with an open cockpit for me to get into and try out. I had expressed to them earlier that I was afraid of getting into and out of my regular kayak because I was no longer as nimble as I once was should I roll over and need to exit the kayak. After a few circles around the dock area in my new kayak, I sensed an uneasiness among those gathered there. They were looking skyward quite often and looking at their watches. What is going on I wondered? Finally, Kristin, my youngest, the ring leader, spoke up and informed me that they had rented a seaplane to come and pick me up at the wharf and take me wherever I wanted to go. The pilot had called her to tell her he was 20 minutes late in leaving Rangeley, but was on his way.

Sure enough a couple of minutes later I saw a bright white seaplane with yellow and red markings, which I had heard earlier, coming around the point below our camp and pulled up right in front of the wharf. It was a 6 passenger Piper so 5 of us climbed in with me in the copilots seat. We took off to the north and headed over Bethel, over the Dartmouth College Grant in Wentworth, then south over Gorham and Dolly Copp campground, viewed Mt. Washington to the West, and then Jackson, the Saco River and then East to Bridgeton and Harrison on our way back to camp. The day was a 50 center – clear, bright, cloudless and calm – a perfect day and a perfect birthday present for one very surprised and pleased 80 year old geezer.

There must have been 15 of us standing around that morning at 7 AM and 14 of them were all clued in to the surprise, but me. They were great at keeping a secret. The CIA needs them.

Dolly Copp Campers Association Decal

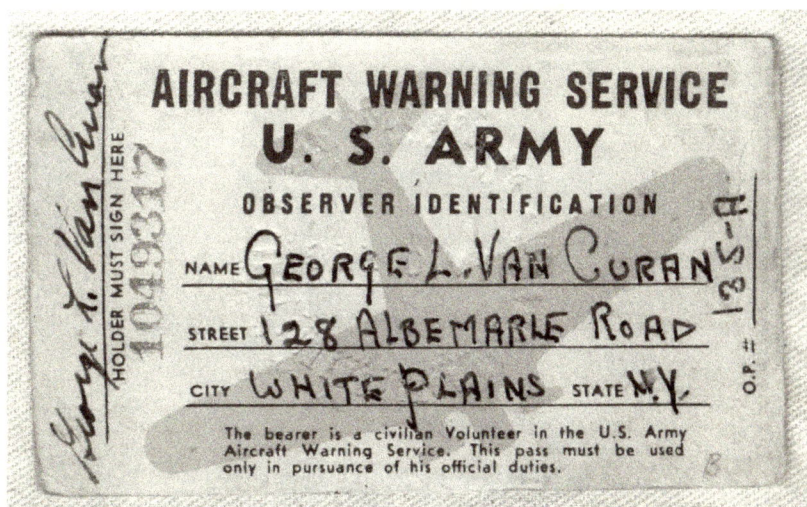

Van's World War II Aircraft Warning Service ID Card

Appalachian Mountain Club Old Hutman's Assn. Decal

White Plains High School Tiger Decal

Mount Washington Observatory Decal

Friends of Tuckerman Ravine Decal

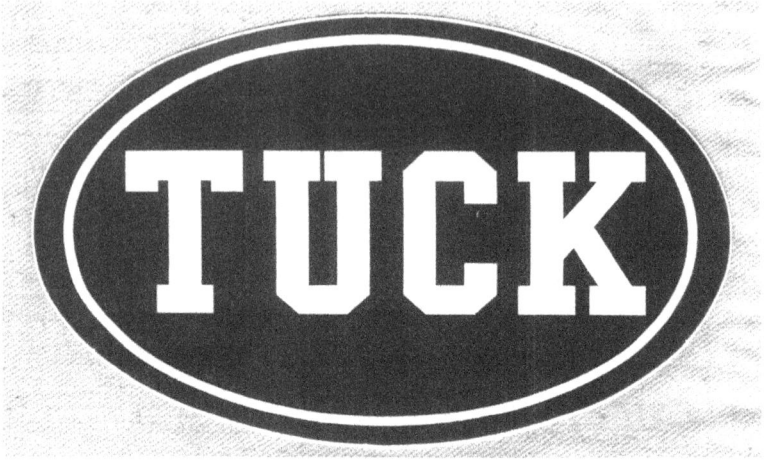

Dartmouth's Amos Tuck School Decal

New England Ski Museum Decal

Sandy's Overseas National Airways Decal

First National Bank Insurance Banking Group

Chris' Selective Service Draft Card

US Army Honorable Discharge Certificate

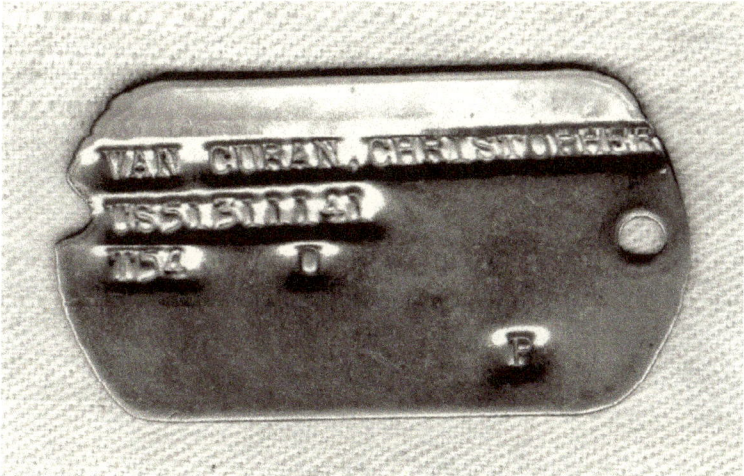

Chris' US Army Dog Tag

Lincoln Fiberglass Canoe Postcard

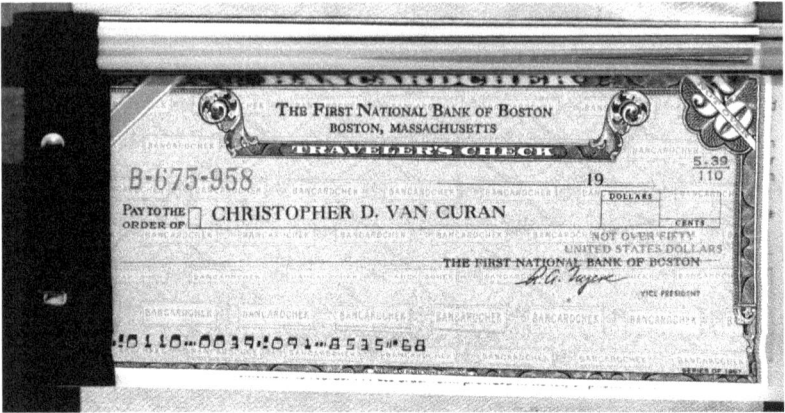

Chris' $50 BanCardChek - Guaranteed Travellers Check

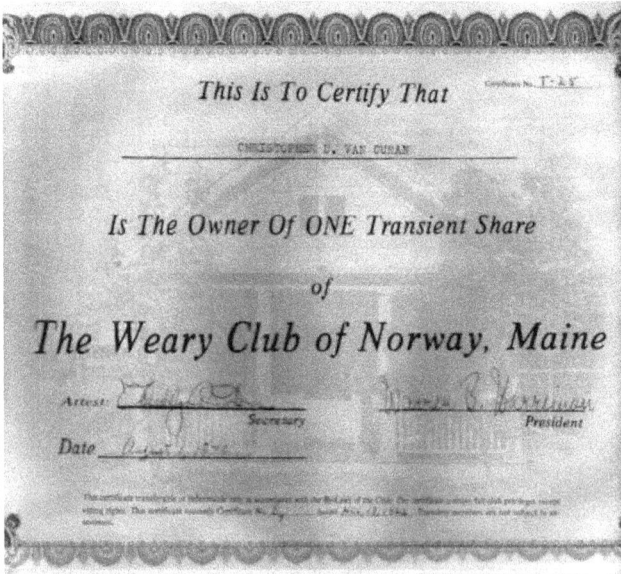

The Weary Club in Norway, Maine

My Memorabilia Box Contents

Over my many decades of life I have kept a memorabilia box. It is a mahogany box 15" long x 7.25" wide and 4.75" deep with a brass handle on top and two brass hinges.

I should probably start at the beginning. Not the beginning of when I started collecting things for this box, but my beginning in life. One of the first items is a cellophane wrapped cigar with the inscription: "Chris Van Curan July 19, 1932 8 lbs. 2 ozs."

This box will go to Peter Johnson, my eldest grandson, when I depart this life. I told him at his 27th birthday party we had camp that I would gift the box to him and that all the stuff in it he did not have to keep because he should start his own collection. And for the start of his collection, I gave him the note that his father, Kevin Johnson, had sent to Sandy and me when he was born twenty-seven years ago.

1949 World Series Baseball Game Ticket
Yankee Stadium. Game 2. Gate 6. Section 19. Box 323B. Seat 7.
This ticket cost $8 for a lower boxstand seat. Daniel Topping was the Yankee President. The Yankees won the series that year.

This ticket stub reminds me of an experience I had some thirty years later. Paul Hardiman and I, both Bank of Boston bankers, were in New York City having an after dinner beer in the P. J. Clark's bar on the other side of the back entrance to the Waldorf Astoria Hotel on Lexington Avenue. We were both sitting at the bar. Across the street in the Waldorf the Sportswriter's black tie dinner had concluded in their ballroom and some of the sportswriter's had come into the bar for another drink before heading home. Behind me I heard a very distinctive voice. It was Mel Allen, the long time radio voice of the NY Yankees and his White Owl cigar advertisements. And, behind Paul, was Red Barber, another long time radio voice of the Brooklyn Dodgers. The two radio icons in baseball oratory and history. Each of them were reaching over us to get their drink orders. While they waited for their drinks to come we chatted for a minute with them. Two baseball icons in one place at the right time for us. Great moment for both of us. Even though both of us were Red Sox fans.

U. S. Army Air Force AWS Observer Arm band, AWS pin and Identification Card

This is a blue and gold arm band worn by Dad during World War II. My Dad volunteered to work for the U. S. Army Air Force as an airplane spotter at night on the Westchester County side of Long Island Sound. He and many others like him spent the whole night in a tower overlooking the Sound looking for enemy aircraft. These volunteers were strung all along the Atlantic Ocean coastline. They had been trained to be able to recognize airplane silhouettes of enemy planes and report them over their telephone connection to a central command center. In return for their service they received extra gas coupons to help defray the cost of commuting to their night job in the tower. I think Dad's tower was in Rye, New York.

Dad's Observer Identification card lists him as 5' 11.5," 170 lbs. brown hair and blue eyes. The pin is a very small pin with Air Force wings and an inscription "Observer" on the lower part.

Cub Scout Neckerchief, Slip Knot, and Shoulder patches

This yellow and blue triangle neckerchief has the cub emblem with the BSA and a cub paw underneath it. The dark blue shoulder patch has "CUBS B.S.A.." The other shoulder patch is "WHITE PLAINS" and "DEN 4."

Boy Scout Merit Badges

I have 17 merit badges all sown together ranging from swimming to birding. There is also a Boy Scout shoulder patch with "WHITE PLAINS" and a "Be Prepared" patch. In addition there are numerous other red merit badges with one being "EC Council BSA Camporee 1945.

Semaphore Signal Flag

This is a white 24"x 24" signal flag with a red 8" x 8" square in the middle of it. It looks like the handiwork of my mother because it is carefully stitched and constructed. As a Boy Scout, I remember tying the flag to a stick and waving it in the precise manner to communicate each Morse Code letter or number to the other communicating party.

Dad's Campus Society Pin 1922

This is a small pin with his initials "G.L.V." engraved on the back. I think it is a college pin. He was the Class of 1921 at Union College in Schenectady, New York.

Reg's Metal Knife Sheath for his belt

It is inscribed "REG.S.DINSMORE, NORWAY,ME." There is no knife that goes with the sheath, but I am sure Reg carried this with him in the woods. It is home made because one edge of the sheath has a leather strip between the two metal pieces and would keep the knife from getting dulled in the sheath. The leather is held in place with 5 small rivets.

Whistle

This whistle I carried with me hunting and fishing in case there was some emergency. It is on a big rubber band attached to my 1981 New Hampshire Resident Hunting & Fishing License. The license is housed in a red plastic case with a clear glassine window so the game warden can see who owns it. I think 1981 is the last year I went hunting in the Dartmouth College Grant with the guys. It cost $14 (fifty cents went to the agent who sold me the license) and I was listed as age 48, 6'3," 185 lbs. and blue eyes. The deer tag is still attached so I did not get a deer that year. I probably brought home a Charlie Brown Christmas tree on the roof of my Subaru wagon.

Book of Waterproof Matches

This is an Army issue of waterproof matches with the inscription on the front: "These matches are designed especially for damp climates, but they will not light when wet, or after long exposure (several weeks) to very damp air.."

BanCardChek

There is a BanCardChek book of checks and an identification card. The checks are "traveler's checks" good for not over specific amount. This was a new product which I helped develop at The First National Bank of Boston in 1968 well before Visa and MasterCard credit cards. It was called "The Everyday Traveler's Check" which Roger Damon, the President of the Bank had invented. This was a guaranteed payment check that was integrated into your personal checking account that allowed you to use these specially printed checks just as if they were "travelers checks." There were a couple of "not over" limits; $50 and $100 limits. Your credit rating with the bank determined which limit was suited to your account. I worked with the American Bank Note Company, DeLuxe Check Printers, and S. D. Warren Paper Company to perfect the checks. S. D. Warren perfected a paper stock with imbedded iridescent chips in the paper that would reflect under ultraviolet light to validate the printed paper, but we ended up not using it because the production run was more expensive and not enough of a production run to make it profitable for them. DeLuxe and American Bank Note printed the checkbooks on that paper in bound books of 10 checks each. So, the credit exposure to the bank ranged from $500 to $1,000, which is not much in today's terms. The project took two years to develop and another year to enlist 120 banks across the United States and Canada to participate on a royalty basis with us. The introduction of plastic credit cards provided an easier and quicker guaranteed transaction payment system. So, BanCardChek became a dinosaur and a vestige of the past.

Passports

My passport issued on November 29, 1977 records me arriving at Gatwick Airport May 10, 1981, Heathrow on December 7, 1981, Heathrow on February 16, 1982, Heathrow on April 19, 1982, Heathrow on September 13, 1982, Hamilton, and Bermuda on November 11, 1982. These entries are when I was with the Bank of Boston and travelling on business to London as part of the Insurance Banking Group, which I headed for the bank.

Sandy's passports are far more interesting and cover the world. Madrid. Grenada. Surabaya. Dominican Republic. Tachikawa. Frankfurt. Aruba. And, of course, Heathrow.

Titanium Surgical Screws

In 1957 I was the first person to break a leg at the newly opened Dartmouth Skiway, also known as "Holts Ledge," under the management of Howie Chivers. It was January 3, 1957 on the Worden Schuss which Walt Praeger, Dartmouth's Alpine Ski Coach, had designed. It was a compound fracture of the left tibia. I had surgery and four screws to secure the tibia. Two at the top of the break and two at the bottom. In 1962 I broke the left leg a second time at Mad River, Vermont which required another surgical procedure. First the leg did not heal (a non-union) since it broke along the lower line of the screws. Four months later I had a bone graft from my iliac crest of my hip and with that operation, the surgeons removed the screws from my leg. These screws are in a gauze wrapper with just a touch of blood on the gauze.

$2 Dollar Bill

$2 dollar bills are called "Race Track" money. They were popular back in the mid-1900's and were the chosen bill for placing bets on race horses at the $2 window. Thomas Jefferson is on the face of the bill.

U. S. Army Dog Tags and Lapel Pins

I have both my dog tags from the Army. "Van Curan, Christopher" on the top line serial number "US51311141" and on the third line "T54," "O" (Blood Type) and on the bottom line "P" (Protestant). I have my "U.S." lapel pins in both silver and brass as well as the U. S. Army insignia pins large and small.

Jim McMullen Matchbox

Sandy and I met at Jim McMullen's restaurant on the Upper East Side of New York City. It was a trendy bar and restaurant catering to the local neighborhood and others, like me, who wanted good food and some atmosphere. I was on a business trip to New York City and decided that evening, since I had no customers to entertain, that I would find a nearby restaurant to get some dinner. Jim McMullen's on Third Avenue caught my eye and I decided to have dinner at the bar. A short time later Sandy and two of her friends (Barbara Stephen and Ruth Perkins) come in with their ONA flight attendant uniforms on and sit next to me. They proceed to order drinks and play "dirty word" scrabble. Being their neighbor at the bar, I could not resist helping their efforts to complete the game. I have the matchbox from that evening.

JG Melon Check Stub, 1291 3ʳᵈ Ave, New York City 212-650-1310

This is the corner bar on Third Avenue and 74ᵗʰ Street. Cab driver instructions would be: "Third Avenue and 74ᵗʰ. Far corner. Right hand side."

This was Sandy's hangout since she lived two blocks up the street from this neighborhood bar. Hal was the first bartender I knew there. He was an actor and roller skated to work. He knew everyone's name and what they drank. He died way too early in life. BC then took over from Hal and was equally as loquacious. They serve the best hamburgers and cottage fries anywhere in New York City. This was the place to go to get a quick meal at the bar. The kitchen is the size of a shoe box. The bar is usually crowded two deep. It is noisy at times. This is where on one early December night I learned that John Lennon had been shot dead over on the West Side. The crowd in the bar hushed at the news. By 11:30PM most everyone had left and gone home they were so saddened and shocked by the news.

Juneta's Birth Certificate

Nettie, as she was known to most of her family, was born on December 29, 1907 in Greenville, Maine. Her record of birth lists her as the first living legitimate birth of Cora Dexter Dinsmore (born in Auburn, Maine) and Regnall Dinsmore (born in Norway, Maine). Reg is listed as a clerk and Cora as a housewife. H. Hunt was the physician in Greenville.

ONA Plastic Swizzle Stick

You would think that this item would have come from Sandy as she worked as a flight attendant for ONA. But, we found it in one of Juneta's kitchen drawers. In the 1970's Juneta and

Tony took a charter flight on ONA to Hawaii with a number of their Maine friends. Juneta, who had an onboard drink kept the swizzle stick in her purse to bring home. It is quite likely that Sandy was one of the flight attendants on that flight though neither could remember if they had met.

Identification Cards

Bank of Boston Authorized Employee Card
Massachusetts Civil Defense as a key worker for The First National Bank of Boston during emergencies.
Original Social Security Card
DD Form 217A – Certificate of Service, Armed Forces of the United States. PFC First Class Christopher D Van Curan US51331141 honorably served on the Active Duty in the Army of the United States.
Sandy's Flight Attendant ID Card for Kennedy International Airport.
Sandy's Association of Flight Attendants Union Card. Member Number: 18228-7. Valid 1/1/79 thru 1/1/83
Sandy's ONA CREW luggage tag. "Sandie Marx, JFK"
Sandy's British Airways name tag. "Sandy Van Curan, Special Services

US Open Tennis Ticket Stubs

Sandy and I went to a few US Open tennis events at the USTA National Tennis Center in Flushing, New York. My son, Dirk, and his wife, Tracey, were hired by American Express to cater their hospitality suite at the Center. They did that event for 15 years.

On September 5, 1991, Sandy and I went to the Thursday night session. We were in the Lower Promenade $30 seats for the night and saw great tennis. I think that was the night that Jimmy Connors and Paul Harhous battled it out until 1AM in breath taking tennis.

On Wednesday night, September 8, 1993 we had $1,800 courtside box seats given to us by my sister and brother-in-law and sat in the VF Corporation box who was a sponsor of the senior events.

Boston Celtics Tickets

In 1983 I financed the purchase of the Boston Celtics from Harry Mangurion. Don Gaston and Paul Dupee, who were my clients, bought the team and then brought in Alan Cohen to complete the acquisition group. They bought the team with $15 million cash ($12 million borrowed from Bank of Boston and $3 of their own) and assumed $6 million of deferred player compensation. Total purchase price was $21 million. A year and a half later they took 40% of their limited partnership public through Smith Barney and created a market capitalization of $132 million. A home run.

With my involvement in the Celtics acquisition Sandy and I had access to all the pre-game receptions in the Celtic's offices and had great seats for the games in "The" Garden. It took about two years to be able to get more permanent seats in Section M, Row 2, Seats 4,5,6,&7. These $28 seats (in 1987) were right behind the Celtic's bench on the floor. I claimed they were "obstructed view" seats because every time the Celtics scored the coach and players would stand up and we could not see the floor.

Pins:

Chi Psi Fraternity Pin

I joined the Chi Psi Fraternity at Middlebury College in the Fall of 1951. On the back of my pin is my whole name (an engraving miracle) "Christopher Van Curan" and A. M. for Alpha Mu. We were called "brothers" and were from many religious faiths and economic backgrounds – Christian, Catholic, Jewish, as well as rich and poor. Some worked for their room and board (me) and others drove Oldsmobiles and wore elegant watches and designer clothes. But we all bonded together as a group and helped each other any way we could. Don Sherburne, three classes ahead of me and a Phi Betta Kappa History Major, pleaded my grade score with Pardon Tillinghast, the history professor, to change my "D" grade of 68 to a "70" so that my 3 "D"s in my first freshman semester would not flunk me out of college. Don succeeded and I stayed in college determined not to let that happen again. It was a tough call home that day I got my failing grades, but an even more pleasant call home a couple of days later with the good news. By the time my senior year came around, I was making honor roll grades.

NASTAR

NASTAR is a skiing competition event held around the United States for amateur skiers to test their racing skills against top ranked alpine skiers. I have a Gold Wildcat NASTAR pin and a silver Snowbird NASTAR pin. Bob Beattie was a strong promoter of this event to get the skiing public into ski racing. Bob was a Middlebury graduate and the last Physical Education major produced at Middlebury. His nickname in college was "Butterbutt," a nickname which Les Streeter pinned him with. Bob along with Jim MacKay broadcast the Wide World of Sports skiing. I think Bob still lives in Aspen.

Other Skiing Pins:

Wildcat Mountain Ski Club

This pin has a big Black "W" on a white background on the left and a perky white wildcat cub face on a red background on the right. And underneath is "Wildcat Mt. Ski Club." I was president of the Wildcat Mountain Ski Club back in the 1970's as well as being on the Board of the Wildcat Mountain Corporation and being their Treasurer. I can remember when Wildcat was being developed in 1956 by Brookie Dodge, Malcolm McLane, George Macomber and Mac Beal. I had just been discharged from the Army in July 1956 and was the Campmaster at Dolly Copp Campground just a couple miles north of the mountain. The trail and lift development work had already started at Wildcat.

NHARA

NHARA (New Hampshire Alpine Racing Association) pin is from when I represented Wildcat Mountain at the Association events. The Association would set the rules and protocols governing the ski racing rules for the junior development programs in the state. It was very political and somewhat influenced by Waterville Valley's Black and Blue Trailsmashers who were the most vocal of the interests in the Association.

Dartmouth Outing Club

I am a lifetime member of the Dartmouth Outing Club and have a couple of DOC pins. One is for 1954-1955 and the other is a green and gold enameled pin with the DOC logo of a snowshoe and crossed skis.

Mt. Tremblant Bronze Pin

In 1968 our whole family went to Mt. Tremblant during the February school vacation week. We stayed in one of the chalets that lined the lower slopes above the main lodge. The chalet we stayed in had a central living room with a fireplace and several bedrooms off each side of the living room. We would trek down to the Main Lodge for all our meals. We were part of a group of five Wayland, Massachusetts families with school age kids on vacation. I got the Mt. Tremblant bronze pin for having a good run on the Flying Mile course at the end of the week's race. My daughter, Kristin, who was 7 at the time, got the real prize however for being the only kid who endured the sub-zero weather to take all the ski lessons we had scheduled that week.

That week is when I also learned from Ernie McCollough's ski school instructors how to ski on ice. Legs and arms farther apart for better balance with subtle motions to turn. One of the instructors that week came down the Flying Mile run on ice skates because it was top to bottom ice.

New England Ski Museum blue and silver pin

The New England Ski Museum in Franconia Notch at the base of Cannon Mountain's Tramway is a treasure of skiing history. We have had an on and off membership there over the years. Susan McLane was one of the founders and we contributed to its creation. Over the years I have collected old ski books from library book sales and yard sales. I probably had a collection of one hundred. I sent a list to the Museum a few years ago to see which ones they would like and they chose about ten of them. One was a Military Handbook on Skiing for the 10th Mountain Division at Camp Hale, Colorado from the 1940's.

1931 – 1981 Daisy Day Ski Club Hochgebirge Pin from Quissett and Ski Club Hochgebirge Pin

The Ski Club Hochgebirge is the oldest alpine ski club in the United States. There are ski clubs in Europe like the Ski Club Arlberg, which are twenty-five years older. And there are Nordic ski clubs older than any alpine club such as the Nansen Club in Berlin, New Hampshire. A number of the Nordic clubs focused on ski jumping as well as cross-country skiing.

The wives of the SCH members were called "Daisies" and in September we would have a Daisy Day event where all the wives and children would come to play games. It was then the only organized family event of the club. The Club also owned a large ski house in Franconia Notch off Coal Hill Road where families could stay. It was called the "Hochie Hilton." The Daisy designation has since disappeared with the Club accepting women as members.

I became a SCH member in 1976. The origin of the club was to attract top ski racers to represent the club in the many competitive club races in New England and the national events around the country. Each club would sponsor a race and trophies would be awarded to the best of the best. I was not one of the top ski racers and never have been a top ski racer. However, I have been very involved in developing junior ski racers in New Hampshire. In 1975 I founded the Wildcat Academy for aspiring junior ski racers, which was a tutorial high school in Jackson, New Hampshire. The Academy allowed a high school student to be tutored in the morning, get bussed to Wildcat Mountain to get lunch and practice on the slopes in the afternoon. Two on the staff were Sheldon and Gardner Perry who were Dartmouth College graduates and top skiers for Dartmouth with Sheldon having been on the US Olympic downhill team. The third staff member was Jeff Graves, a UNH ski team member who taught the sciences and math.

High School Football Pins

I have two White Plains High School football pins for being the Manager of the team in 1948 and 1949. Inscribed on the pins is "C.Van C." I was not big nor strong enough to play football. I was probably 6 feet tall, but only weighed 140 or so pounds. I was responsible for getting all the uniforms cleaned and accounted for, all the equipment ready to use on the field like practice balls, towels, drinks, etc. The supply room with t-shirts and other athletic equipment was under my control.

Church Perfect Attendance Pins

I have three perfect attendance pins. I know this will probably surprise those of you who know me. I only step in to a church to attend a memorial service these days. Two indicate 9 months perfect attendance and the third is a silver and green perfect attendance pin. These came from the Congregational Church in

White Plains, New York and Reverend Eliezer Wheelock was the Pastor. My parents were raising me to be a good Christian. My mother identified with the Universalist Unitarian Church and I really don't recall if my Dad identified with any particular Christian religion. But, my sister and I went to church school regularly every Sunday.

Mount Washington Observatory Membership Cards

I have been a member of MWOBS for over 50 years dutifully paying membership dues in order to keep supporting their meteorological efforts on the summit but also to get their quarterly "Windswept" mini-magazine which has some feature story about the mountain plus all the last quarter's weather data. It has always been an interesting read. The Observatory, which was founded in 1932 by Joe Dodge, Bob Monahan and a couple of others, has had a rocky and challenging history.

Back in the 1970's the local savings bank sponsored a radio weather program at 6:45AM for the school kids about to get off for school. I think it was Mac Beal's Mt. Washington Savings Bank that was the sponsor and gave out piggy banks to the school kids. The program would start with Skip Sherman, the radio announcer, getting Joe Dodge on the phone, who would get the report of the weather from the summit, Pinkham Notch and the Valley. Joe had been a trained radio signal operator in the Navy and carried that over to being a ham radio operator when he got out of the service. If the weather was judged to be spectacular for the day, Joe would call it a "50 center." If it was to be an ugly rainy, snowy miserable day, he would call it a "5 center." Nothing above 50 cents and nothing below 5 cents. And the listeners, school children and parents would throw whatever coins were necessary to reflect the call of the day into the Mt. Washington Savings piggy bank. At the end of the year when counting up the change, you had a statistical quantitative judgment of the past year's weather. Good year compared to last or whatever. Briggs Bunker carried on the weather program after Joe retired in the 1980's.

The OH Association Membership Cards

The Old Hutman's Association is a membership group of hutmen who worked in the Appalachian Mountain Club huts for thirteen or more consecutive weeks. This could include work at Lonesome Lake, the westernmost hut in Franconia Notch, or the old Evan's Notch "hut" to the East or Pinkham Notch, the year round "Trading Post." In the 1950's it also included those AMC staff that worked at Dolly Copp Campground of which I was one of them. I qualified for membership after my first summer there and I would take days off to visit the huts. My favorite hut was and still is Carter Notch. "Cozy Carter" was the term I used to describe it. Paul Dougherty, the Fish and Game Warden also known as the "fish cop," filled an Indian firefighting water tank with brook trout, which he strapped to his back and stocked the lake or tarn at Carter. I would often take my "trunk" fly rod with me into Carter to fish the lake. A "trunk" rod is a five section fly rod, which I inherited from my father who was also an avid fisherman.

I am also proud to say that my grandson, Anders Nordblom, is an OH member from having worked summers at Mispah and Greenleaf huts while at Colby College.

White Plains High School Ring 1950

This is your classic traditional high school ring. White Plains High School was considered a very good academic school. Ms. Savage was my Latin Teacher. Bessie Cudworth, a Middlebury graduate, was my English teacher and urged me to apply to Middlebury. Not for my English skills I am sure. Alva Otis was our classics and ancient history teacher. He had a cleft lip which created a slight speech impairment but he knew his subject. Mrs. Sweetman was my algebra teacher and she was anything but. She gave boys in her class lower grades than the girls. Or, at least, that was my impression. I was struggling with a high C grade in her algebra class and the New York State regents exams were coming up which everyone was required to take. I studied hard for those exams to improve my grade since she could do nothing to change or influence that exam grade. I got a very high result and she was forced to give me a B+.

Our team mascot was the Tiger. So we were the orange and black White Plains Tigers. Our football coach was Glenn Loucks, a Syracuse All-American. In 1947 I was a freshman in high school. The war had ended two years before and the war veterans were returning home. Many of them enlisted before they finished high school so now were coming back to complete their high schooling. White Plains had a number of these boys, now men, returning and playing sports. The football program benefitted the most. Our league comprised many of the surrounding cities and beyond so we played Yonker's A.B. Davis, New Rochelle, Port Chester, Hempstead, Hamden (CT), Salem (MA), Hershey (PA) and Alliance (OH). Dick Nolan went on to the University of Maryland, played professionally and then became Tom Landry's Assistant Coach for the Dallas Cowboys and Head Coach of the San Francisco 49er's. Frank Navarro, who also played professionally, ended up as the long time football coach for Williams College.

Grandmother Ede's Silver Retirement Jewelry Box

The top lid of the box is inscribed; "Edith L. Van Curan, From your Canco Friends, May 29, 1941. She had worked at Canco for many years in Rochester, New York.

In this light green velvet lined sterling silver box is a gold locket pendent with two pictures. It may be a baby picture of Dad on one side and on the other side his father (Ede's husband). The outside has very scripted initials which are hard to decipher. Then there are some coins, a gold wedding band and in a black leather pouch with gold inscription "L. G. Balfour Co., Attleboro, Mass. holds my Dad's Beta Theta Pi fraternity pin and a pin on a gold chain.

Decals

Dolly Copp Campers Association, Gorham, NH
Mount Washington Observatory 1932 – 1982
White Plains Tigers
Overseas National Airways
New England Ski Museum, Franconia, NH
The OH Association
Friends of Tuckerman Ravine, Est. 2000
TUCK for the Amos Tuck School of Business Administration

Postcards and Notes
Friends of Hockey, Dartmouth College, Membership #492
Honorary Membership in the Swiss Army Knife Society,

December 9, 1991. Bob Craven was also a Swiss Army Knife aficionado. Whenever we visited them in Franconia, NH Bob and I would have a contest as to who had more blades and tools on their Swiss army knife. One year I went into the Stoddard's store on Temple Place in Boston to inquire about other small tools that go with a Swiss army knife as I told them about the contest we were having. They suggested an eye glass screw driver which was able to be screwed into the cork screw tool. I bought two of them. I mounted one in my knife and kept the other awaiting the next knife contest with Bob. Sure enough I won the next event by that one tool, so I gave Bob the second eye glass screw driver and we have been even ever since.

Jim McMullen (Restaurant), 1341 Third Avenue, New York, NY 10021 (212) 861-4700.

I met Sandy at this restaurant. She, Barbara Stephen and Ruth Perkins came in to the restaurant after having come in off a trip from somewhere. The three of them decided to eat at the bar and took seats next to me. I was eating dinner at the bar. We struck up a conversation and the rest is history.

The First National Bank of Boston, Insurance Group Card.

Listing of our staff in Boston, New York, and London.

Lincoln Fiberglass Canoe Division of The Lazott Company, Inc., Westboro, Mass.

"Tony Be right back J"

This is the note my mother kept forever on her front door at home. She thought this note was her security system.

Transient Member card for The Weary Club of Norway, Maine signed by Franklyn Towne and Warren B. Harriman dated August 1, 1979.

Given to me by Tony Allen, my step-father.

**Norway Fire Department Alarm Box and Location Card.
Box Number and Street. Norway Lake was 115.**

Robert Butters was Fire Chief.

South Paris Fire Alarm Boxes. Box Number and Street.

Fire Chief was Harold R. Edwards. Printed by Stony Brook Print Shop.

Norway Mileage Chart.

Mileage to other cities and towns in Maine. Portland – 46 miles; Bethel – 25 miles; Kittery – 97 miles; Fort Kent – 387 miles; Bar Harbor – 160 miles. Printed by Stony Brook Print Shop

Juneta's List of Bequests to Jean and me.

Nettie had two lists which she kept later in life in her diary. One was a list of the things which Jean would inherit after her death and the second was a similar list of items for me. I got the Towne antique desk and the March Sunlight painting and Jean got a grandfather clock and the painted portrait of Juneta, both paintings by V. Akers. Juneta's portrait recalls an interesting story. My dad was a member of the Salmagundi Club in New York City which held regular luncheon meetings with guest speakers. Sometime around 1953 Chief Justice Earl Warren came to speak.

After the lunch was over Dad was speaking with the Chief Justice who said he had just commissioned a Maine artist to paint his portrait to hang in the Hall of Justices in Washington, DC. He complained that it had been taking the artist, V. Akers in Norway, Maine an awful long time to get the painting started because he was painting a portrait of some "damn woman." Dad replied that that "damn woman" was his wife, Juneta.

Coins and Medals
Silver Dollar on a silver chain. Coin dated 1894

Silver Dollar Hotel, Denver, Colo, "Good for one screw," Madame Ruth Jacobs Prop. $3 All night Check. Never used. What is it worth today?

1888 Banff Hotel Centennial 1988, Banff Alberta Canada Mount Rundle 1988

$20 1988 Calgary Olympic Winter Game coin in a green velvet box.

Annie and Kevin gave me this for my birthday in 1988.

Saint Christopher Protect Us Medal
Flying Wings.

Don't recognize the logo emblem on the front. May have been Uncle Sam Chandler's. Sam Chandler was my mother's sister's husband. He grew up in the Portland area and learned to fly airplanes at an early age. He flew the US Mail from Portland to Bangor to Boston and back. He later went on the fly for Northeast Airlines, which got acquired by Eastern Airlines. During the war Sam flew for the Military Air Transport Command Service (MATS). MATS ferried bombers, like B-17's and B-24's to Russia from Miami to Belem to Africa to Cairo to Tehran to Moscow. Then one plane would fly everyone back to the states. He spent his life flying. He was also a gifted piano player when he had at least one scotch in him.

US Army issue can opener

This is a unique small metal can opener which you could attach to your dog tag chain. It is collapsible and has a hinged cutting blade that provides the cutting edge for opening canned goods. So much of the field rations during the war were in cans that this tool became invaluable to the soldiers fighting on the front lines.

Boy Scouts of America. War Savings Service. Ace.

Presented on behalf of the National War Savings Committee for service in the War Savings Campaign. 1918. On a red-white-blue ribbon metal with an oak leaf cluster.

Patches and Bags
Norway National Bank, Norway, Maine.

Coin and Currency bag made by Porter Safety Seal Co., Chicago

College Athletic Letter "R."

I think this is an athletic letter award to Dad for baseball when he went to the University of Rochester before he transferred to Union College. It is yellow stitched over dark blue purple felt.

Assortment of military patches and rank chevrons.

I collected these during World War II. One is particularly interesting. I was told that the blue gray shoulder epaulet "28" was cut off a dead German soldiers uniform during World War I. The only family member I think that served in that war was Uncle Frank Raymond and it may have come from him.

My Carter Notch Hut patch.

This deserves some mention. I got this on my 79th birthday as a gift from Anders Nordblom, my grandson, and Molly Muller, Ander's girlfriend. Molly was hutmaster at Carter and knew she was coming to my birthday party at camp with Anders.

Cassette Tape Recording
Harry Harpers Eulogy to Juneta Dinsmore Allen, Lane 18,

Norway Lake, July 7, 1990 – 1 side

Dr. Harper is a close family friend and was Nettie's primary care physician for many years. He had a private practice in South Paris and was on the medical staff at Stephens Memorial Hospital for years where the Medical Center building is named after him. He loves jazz and ragtime music which is a lifelong hobby to collect 78rpm recordings and transfer them to cassettes. He would buy them at yard sales and library book sales all over Maine. One of his great pleasures was to make a copy for you which is accomplished by dropping a very slight hint that you liked a particular piece of music. It didn't take much of a hint either. Evelyn, his 95 year old wife, was a frequent golfing partner with Nettie at the Norway Country Club and played into her 90's. About 10 years ago Dr. Harper wrote a book about his medical practice in a small Maine town and titled it "Dr. Iodine." It was a pleasant read, but some of us felt that he should keep his "day" job.

SO – How is that for memories from a box. It is like letting a Genie out of a bottle who can tell it all.

The Memorabilia Box is kind of like this book. Random material with interesting stories behind them.

I have enjoyed writing this book, which has spanned some 25 odd years. It has been a labor of love.

Hope you enjoyed it – in part or in it's entirety.

www.ingramcontent.com/pod-product-compliance
Lightning Source LLC
Chambersburg PA
CBHW031839090426
42741CB00005B/293